ALSO BY SANJAY GUPTA

12 WEEKS *to a* SHARPER YOU

A Guided Program

Based on the #1 *New York Times* Bestselling Book *Keep Sharp*

Sanjay Gupta, MD

with Kristin Loberg

SIMON & SCHUSTER PAPERBACKS

New York London Toronto Sydney New Delhi

THIS WORKBOOK BELONGS TO:

_____

START DATE:

_____

DATE OF COMPLETION:

_____

CONTENTS

CONTENTS

PART TWO • A GUIDED TOUR OF THE KEEP SHARP PROGRAM WEEK BY WEEK

The chief function of the body . . .
is to carry the brain around.

—Thomas Edison

For my three girls, Sage, Sky, and Soleil. In order of age, so as to preempt any future disputes over the dedication order. I love you so much, and watched you grow faster than this book. Always take the time to be completely present, because it is perhaps the best and most joyous way to keep your mind sharp and your life bright. You are still so young, yet you have given me a lifetime of memories I hope to never forget.

For my Rebecca, who has never wavered in enthusiasm. If in the end, our lives are just a collection of memories, mine will be filled of images of your beautiful smile and your steadfast support.

For anybody who has dreamed that their brain can be better. Not just free of disease or trauma, but optimized in a way that allows you to best build and remember your life narrative, and equips you to be resilient through life's challenges. For anyone who has always believed their brain wasn't a black box, impenetrable and untouchable, but could be nourished and grown into something greater than they imagined.

12 WEEKS *to a* SHARPER YOU

INTRODUCTION
A CALL TO PUT YOU—
AND YOUR BRAIN—FIRST

Welcome! And congratulations in advance. You're only twelve weeks away from carrying around a better brain that has enormous potential to stay sharp for the rest of your life. No matter how old you are, the good news is it's never too late to make a positive difference in how well your brain functions as the years tick by and you age. It's an incredibly responsive organ to our habits—an organ that we can improve on with the right choices. Indeed, your brain can be nourished and grown into something greater than you've ever imagined. And that's something that should motivate you to establish the habits that will keep you sharp for life. There's nothing brainy about it—anyone can build a better brain at any age. Whether you're twenty-two or ninety-two, you've come to the right place.

We used to think that we were born with a certain cache of neurons that would slowly deplete over our life. We were told substances like alcohol could accelerate that process, and there was no coming back. Keep in mind that most of these outdated notions were based on observations of the brain during a diseased state. For a long time, we only saw the brain at the time of autopsy—after its occupier was dead. This is how Alois Alzheimer first found the telltale plaques of the disease named after him at the turn of the twentieth century. And, up until recently, it was still only through an autopsy that a family member could be told of the Alzheimer's diagnosis with certainty. As a neurosurgeon, I hardly ever look at healthy brains, but rather ones invaded by a tumor, filled with blood, or crushed by trauma. Point is, we have just begun to quantify the healthy brain. And that's critical because to maintain and improve a healthy brain, we must understand it as best we can.

Once we started to look at healthy brains, our fundamental understanding began to change. We saw the brain grow and regenerate not to repair damage, but rather to get . . . better. And better. And better. We now know the brain can reliably revamp itself and be continuously optimized throughout one's life. We know the brain has a rinse cycle and can even predict when that cycle is most likely to occur—sleep.[1] We can tell when you are most likely to be productive and creative, and when you are starting to redline on the verge of burnout. We can confirm that what is good for the heart is often good for the brain, but not always. Most exciting, there is now substantial evidence that you can grow new brain cells *at any age*.[2] Think about that. You can spawn new brain cells and form new connections whether you're a teddy-bear-toting toddler, trailblazing twentysomething, or tennis-loving centenarian. It's not nearly as challenging as you might think, but it does require some conscientious effort and planning. Anything worthy of monumental change demands that, plus some patience and perseverance. But you can also have fun along the way and learn new things that will surprise—and entertain—you.

After all, we are talking about maintaining and improving the most enigmatic three and a half pounds of flesh in the known universe. It is the world's most sophisticated, self-propagating supercomputer, with a parallel operating system known as consciousness. So, yes: We should take the necessary time to care for this critical system, keep it shiny and full of the right fuel for it to truly run on the bumpy road of life without consequence.

As you dive into this new workbook updated with the latest science, I want you to consider a fundamental question: What is a healthy brain? Sure, we can well define a healthy heart. Same goes for the liver, kidneys, even your spleen. But the brain? Many will say that a healthy brain is one devoid of cancer, trauma, stroke, or plaque that interrupts communication and destroys memory. However, that is defining health as simply the absence of disease. We must go further. We must be more ambitious.

A healthy brain not only manages memory well but it also connects patterns that would otherwise be missed. Those patterns are what facilitate and further bolster the brain's memory-making and banking. A healthy brain is also one that is not easily crushed by the tough, stressful toll of daily life, but is instead strengthened by it.

We often think of a fit brain as one that can remember details well, but it is worth reconsidering this definition. What is memory anyway? We often think of it as a precise journal of past life events that we flip through like a Rolodex or filing cabinet (or maybe you see the comparison to scrolling through photos stored in your online digital cloud). From an evolutionary perspective, memory has served to recall situations, people, and sources of food and water to help protect and sustain life. But we now appreciate memory for its most powerful purpose: to reinforce our own life's narrative, the story of us. And sometimes our memories aren't entirely accurate but that's okay.

Truth is, within a given day, we probably pay attention to only 60 to 70 percent of all that's in front of us. Because the rest of our daily experience doesn't necessarily fill or contribute to the way we see our life's narrative, we ignore it. That means a healthy brain is one that remembers the important things, while at the same time forgets the trivial. And yes, forgetting is just as important as remembering, and can even help us sharpen our brains and make room for new—and more valuable—information. Scientists only discovered our "forgetting" neurons in 2019 in a groundbreaking study that further revealed the importance of sleep, a time period when these specialized brain cells spring into action.[3] It's a beautiful paradox: In order to remember, we have to forget to some extent. As the wonderful evolutionary biologist Robert Sapolsky told me, a healthy brain is also one that has a wide circle of "you"—a brain inclusive to new ideas and new people. A brain less dismissive, and more welcoming.

As an academic neurosurgeon and a reporter, I educate and explain. I am a firm believer in explaining *what* and *why*. Once you understand the inner workings of the brain, the specific habits I recommend will make sense. If I simply tell you what you should do, you are less likely to adopt the habit. If you truly understand why the recommendation will help your brain, you now have a story to recall and follow. This book is that story.

Since the first publication of *Keep Sharp* in 2021, I have been delighted to learn the impact it has had on people around the world. My colleague Erin Burnett has taken up painting to successfully help build cognitive reserve, a concept I'll define shortly. An eighty-seven-year-old woman from Bangkok emailed me to share her joy over her newfound cognitive prowess—more thinking power, faster recall, and overall better mental energy. And a fortysomething father with a tiring juggle between parenting young children and supporting aging parents who felt mentally recharged and energized by slightly shifting his food choices, ending his soda fix, and prioritizing sleep. So many of you shared your own stories after following the twelve-week program in the book that it became the inspiration for this new interactive workbook. As promised in *Keep Sharp* and again in this workbook, it is important that you know there are no gimmicks here—only true self-discovery rooted in the best available science.

To that end, let me be clear that there's no formula here to end dementia or magically reverse someone who is in decline. Some of you may be coming to this book with cognitive challenges or even a condition like mild cognitive impairment (MCI), which often precedes a more serious diagnosis like dementia. Or perhaps you or someone in your family is suffering from a severe neurodegenerative disease that has progressed from a mild state. The strategies in this workbook are designed to give you the best chance of optimizing your brain health, and while this endeavor may slow the progression of a disease in some individuals, no one can offer a guaranteed remedy to any brain ailment. The complexity of brain conditions makes the protection of peak brain function all the more important, at any age. Don't give up if you or a loved one has cognitive issues. The more you work on improving your brain, the more you stand to gain in prolonging your brain's health over your lifetime and managing any brain-related ailment if that's a reality. So, while there are parts to brain health that are beyond anyone's control, there are things you can be doing today to support the best possible neural network for your future.

I began my *Keep Sharp* project working with AARP in 2017, soon after the longtime organization launched the independent collaborative called the Global Council on Brain Health (GCBH). The GCBH brings experts from around the world together to debate the latest in brain health science and reach consensus on what works and doesn't work. Its goal is to help people apply scientific insights to promote better brain health as they age. We share the vision that there is no one answer, magic pill, or silver bullet when it comes to brain health (despite what some advertisers and unscrupulous marketers will tell you). When you search "how to improve brain health" online, it doesn't take much scrolling to come across suspect sites selling all kinds of questionable ideas with no scientific data to support their products. Caveat emptor: There is no such thing as a pill you can swallow to "improve memory," "sharpen focus," or "prevent dementia" no matter how convincing the claims may be (and yet a quarter of adults over age fifty are taking a supplement to try to keep their brains healthy).

Instead, what you need to know is that it's never too early or too late to try to improve your brain health, and that you can reduce your risks for cognitive decline by adopting healthy behaviors across your life span. And many of those behaviors don't cost a thing other than a little committed effort. Recently, in "How to Sustain Brain Healthy Behaviors: Applying Lessons of Public Health and Science to Drive Change," the GCBH set out the three foundational elements necessary for people to implement this lifestyle: knowledge, motivation, and confidence.[4] I will spend a lot of time sharing what we know with full transparency, giving you the knowledge and providing you with the motivation and confidence that you can apply this in your life to make a difference now and for the future.

I've divided this workbook into two parts. In Part One, "What It Means to Keep Sharp for Life," I provide a refresher course on the 6 main categories to protect and maintain brain health: 1) nutrition; 2) movement (not just "exercise"); 3) downtime (in waking hours); 4) restorative sleep; 5) discovery; and 6) connection. You'll find that I've split the original "Downtime" pillar described in *Keep Sharp* into two distinct pillars for the workbook (hence, 6 rather than 5 pillars here). There's a difference between what you do to rest, destress, and relax during waking hours and how you achieve rejuvenating sleep consistently at night. Both are important forms of recovery but command slightly different skill sets. For further details about the science behind all these pillars, *Keep Sharp* remains a highly useful, well-researched, and fully cited resource (new citations are listed at the back of this workbook; some language in these pages is adapted from *Keep Sharp* with relevant updates and additions). Part Two breaks down the program into 12 weeks, with each week focusing on one or two aspects of the 6 pillars. I'll provide the stepping stones, so to speak, and you merely have to put one foot in front of the other and make your way.

As scientists continue to study the many pathways that can lead to dementia, including Alzheimer's, one thing remains abundantly clear: No single trigger or cause has been found. Many events and biological circumstances can cause cognitive decline and disease, and even the long-held belief that amyloid-beta plaques in the brain are the main culprit is under further scrutiny. Just as there are many roads that can lead to cancer, many roads lead to Alzheimer's. According to Dr. Richard Isaacson, a pioneer in preventive therapies for dementia, each person's journey is uniquely different. "There is a saying," he reminds me. "Once you have seen one person with Alzheimer's, you've seen one person with Alzheimer's." He has objectively improved cognition in his patients starting by simply targeting "weak spots" that could be upping their risk for—or contributing to—cognitive decline. Those weak spots are often easy to address with lifestyle choices or, when necessary, certain medications. The goal is to help gain strict control over things like cholesterol or blood pressure, which can have a heavy hand not only on heart disease but also on brain health.

Regardless of the debates and studies that are ongoing, always remember this: **Cognitive decline is not necessarily inevitable.** Research suggests healthy habits you can incorporate into your daily life can help protect your brain health for the long term. And a multifaceted approach to preserving—and optimizing—brain function and health is essential. As an analogy, think of a historic building that still stands strong. Perhaps it's more than a century old. Had it not been cared for throughout the decades, the wear and tear of time and constant use would have certainly caused its deterioration and dilapidation. But with routine maintenance and occasional renovations, it not only withstood the test of time but is likely celebrated for its beauty, significance, and prominence. The same holds true for your brain, which is a biological structure that requires maintenance and upkeep in many forms. To combat a constellation of events that lead to brain decline, you need to deploy an arsenal of brain-buttressing forces. Those forces are exactly what encompass this program.

Some of the activities in this workbook will help assemble brain scaffolding—creating a support structure for your brain that is stronger and more stable than what you currently have and will help you to perform some initial "renovations," reinforcing your brain's "foundation." Other strategies will provide the raw materials necessary for ongoing maintenance, as well as build what's called "cognitive reserve," which is what scientists call "brain resiliency." With more cognitive reserve, you can lower your risk of developing dementia. It's like having a backup set of networks in your brain when one fails or, worse, dies and is no longer functional. In many aspects of life, the more backup plans we have, the more chances for success, right? Well, the same is true for our brain's hard- and softwiring. Finally, there will be lessons to apply daily touches akin to dusting and tidying up to keep the brain performing optimally. As I mentioned, the old-school thinking dictated that the brain was pretty much fixed and unalterable after childhood development. People believed—and some still do—this mysterious organ encased in bone is a black box of sorts, untouchable and incapable of being improved. Not true. Today, as we visualize the brain with new imaging technologies and study its ever-changing function, we know otherwise.

You are not necessarily doomed to whatever fate you think sits stuck in your genes. If there's one fact that's increasingly becoming apparent in scientific circles, it's that our lifestyle choices contribute mightily to our aging process and risk for disease—likely as much or perhaps even more so than our genetics. Indeed, your everyday experiences, including what you eat, how much you move, with whom you socialize, what challenges you face, what gives you a sense of purpose, how well you sleep, and what you do to reduce stress, factor much more into your brain health and overall wellness than you can imagine. A landmark 2018 study, published in the journal *Genetics*, revealed that the person we marry factors more than our genetic inheritance into our longevity.[5] And by a long shot! Why? Because it turns out that our lifestyle decisions such as whom we choose to spend our life with weigh heavily into our well-being—much more so than most other factors in our lives. Worry less about your genes and stop using them as an excuse. Instead, focus on the things you get to choose, big and small, day in and day out. Clean living can slash your risk of developing a serious mind-destroying disorder, including Alzheimer's disease, even if you carry genetic risk factors. No matter what your DNA says, a good diet, regular movement, not smoking, limiting alcohol, social engagement, and other surprising lifestyle decisions can change that destiny.

As of 2022, scientists have documented a total of about seventy-five genes connected to the development of Alzheimer's, but carrying these genes is not a one-way ticket to decline.[6] How those genes express themselves and *behave* may depend largely on your daily habits. Remember that a disease like Alzheimer's is multifactorial, made up of different pathological features. Which is why prevention and treatments are increasingly becoming personalized—individualized to a person's biochemistry, from basic parameters like cholesterol levels, blood pressure, and blood sugar balance, to the state of one's oral health and gut microbiome, relics of past infections, and even molecular signals in one's genomics. As noted above, DNA provides your body's core language, but how that DNA behaves tells the story. In the future, interventional therapies that include a combination of lifestyle habits and drugs may help those stories end well.

Although we hear disheartening news in the media about failed drug trials for dementia, the good news is precision medicine is moving fast in this area. In the future, you'll track your risk for cognitive decline over time using a simple app on your smartphone that can help you evaluate your physiology (and your memory!) in real time and make suggestions tailored for you. Until we all have that technology at our fingertips, this workbook is a great start and will give you a strong foundation.

In 2022, a large study that tracked the health of more than half a million people showed that the simple act of performing household chores like cooking, cleaning, and washing the dishes can cut the risk of dementia by a stunning 21 percent.[7] That put chores as the second biggest protective activity behind more obvious things such as brisk walking and riding a bike, and we ought to pay attention to these basic and doable lessons. In this same study, regular movement was shown to reduce risk for dementia by 35 percent, followed by meeting up with friends and family (15 percent lower risk). Again, simple things with huge payoffs. I like an adage I once heard in Okinawa: "I want to live my life like an incandescent light bulb. Burn brightly my entire life, and then one day suddenly go out." There should be no flickering at the end. We want the same for our brains.

As you actively use this workbook, it's perfectly fine to go at your own pace, and I hope you make the steps personal for your success. You can take as many weeks as you need to adopt and establish new habits until they become embedded in your daily life. For example, you can stretch the first week's lessons and activities out for two or three weeks. Do what's necessary for your own success here. If you feel changes starting to take hold, continue to follow those recommendations and make them a habit. After all, this is about you and your life. At whatever tempo you go, do not rush the process. Remember that this is a journey of a thousand miles with infinite destinations. Be patient with yourself and feel free to tailor my suggestions to your preferences so long as they remain within reasonable confines of what we know is healthy.

If there's one fact I've learned in my years of studying the brain, operating on brains, and working with top scientists, it's that each of us carries our own unique profile. That is why any program to improve brain health needs to be wide-ranging, evidence-based, inclusive, and flexible. And while there is no one-size-fits-all solution (don't believe anyone who tells you otherwise), there are simple interventions all of us can make right away that can have a significant impact on our cognitive function and long-term brain health. To that end, I also ask that you be intentional, diligent, and courageous as you move forward. I want this workbook to be yours and yours alone. While you can certainly go through this program with a friend (and I do think that's a great idea), make this workbook your own personal document of your journey. I'm excited to be your guide and your teacher.

For most of us, our brains are probably working at half capacity at any given time. Sure, it's an estimated guess because there's no way to know what that figure is for any given individual, but it seems reasonable. Regardless, you can optimize your brain far more than you probably realize or appreciate and the vast majority of people haven't even begun to try. I think all of us would do well to put more focus on our brain health just as we do other important things in life like watching our weight or raising our children. Aside from lowering your risk for brain disease, think about all the other perks that come with better brain health—experiencing less anxiety and depression, being more productive and present, and navigating through life with ease, energy, and joy.

I'll be asking you to write down your personal goals and wishes for going through this program, but I think the goals I just mentioned are ones we all can appreciate and strive to obtain. I've had the privilege of going to specialists all over the world to get insights and action plans to keep my brain sharp and prevent decline. I've been sharing this knowledge with everyone I hold near and dear to me. Now I want the same for you. Since I began to write *Keep Sharp*, the world has changed immensely in its tenor and state of affairs. We've all gone through a once-in-a-lifetime pandemic, watched shifts in social and cultural norms, and faced unprecedented challenges. Some of you may be experiencing long Covid, which we know can have neurological consequences. I've got some ideas for you coming up in the program as well. There's never been a more essential time to work on our brains to think more critically and clearly, to make better decisions for ourselves and loved ones, and to connect more intimately with others.

Thank you for trusting me and allowing me to steer you in the direction of vibrant brain health and function. You deserve to have the best brain possible. And it's within your reach. I know it. You do too, which is why you're here.

Now let's get going . . .

PART ONE

WHAT IT MEANS TO KEEP SHARP FOR LIFE

Our brains determine who we are and the world we experience. They allow us to perceive joy and wonder, and develop vital connections with others. They shape our identity and give us a sense of self. We also rely on our brains to make good decisions, plan, and prepare for the future. They even tells stories in the form of dreams when we're sleeping. And they know how to adapt to environments, tell time, and shape memories.

Overall, the human brain is the most complex object known in the universe—known, that is, to itself.
—Edward O. Wilson

The brain is exceptionally "plastic"—it's not immutable.[1] It can "bend" and rewire itself in response to its environment, which rests largely on how you choose to live your life.[2] And that plasticity is a two-way street. In other words, it's almost as easy to drive changes that impair memory and cognition as it is to improve them. You can change your brain for better or worse through behaviors and ways of thinking. Bad habits create neural paths that reinforce those bad habits. Negative thoughts and constant worrying can promote changes in the brain that are associated with depression and anxiety. On the flip side, positivity and healthful behaviors can support optimal brain function and fortify the networks you want to keep. Repeated mental states, where you focus your attention, what you experience, and how you respond to situations become neural traits.

This is a concept known as the Hebbian learning rule.[3] It is often described by neuroscientists as an idea that "neurons wire together, if they fire together." We know the connections between neurons have the ability to change like molded plastic, and those modifications, both good and bad, are continuously happening based on our own behavioral patterns and experiences. The good news is that you are more in control of the way your neurons are firing and wiring than you probably realize. Even as you simply read this page, think, and feel the sense of empowerment you have over the supercomputer in your skull, your brain is changing, for the better.

Of all the offenders that can damage the brain and raise risk for neurodegeneration and cognitive decline, the most egregious one is a biological process you've probably heard about by now: inflammation. More specifically, chronic inflammation associated with aging ("inflamm-aging") is at the center of nearly all degenerative conditions, from those that increase one's risk for dementia, such as diabetes and vascular diseases, to those that are directly brain-related, such as depression and Alzheimer's disease.[4] For decades scientists debated the role of inflammation in a diseased brain, but now a burst of new research suggests that inflammation not only adds to disease processes in the brain that cause decline but also triggers those processes in the first place. Studies that have come out in the last few years have shown that chronic inflammation at midlife is linked to later cognitive decline and Alzheimer's disease.[5] Although inflammation is useful in the body to defend against injury and invaders, it becomes a problem when that system is constantly activated and releasing chemical substances and keying up the immune system. Think of a fire hose that's turned on to put out a flame but then never gets shut off. All that water that was once helpful and restorative is now destructive.

As formerly promising drugs continue to fail in clinical trials to prevent or treat dementia, the narrative around the disease is changing. In 2020, the influential *Lancet* released its updated report on dementia prevention, intervention, and care.[6] The report, which was originally published in 2017 by a panel of doctors, epidemiologists, and public health experts, listed the following nine risk factors: less education, high blood pressure, hearing impairment, smoking, obesity, depression, physical inactivity, diabetes, and low social contact. In 2020, the report added three more risk factors with new substantial evidence: excessive alcohol consumption, traumatic brain injury, and air pollution. The authors made a stunning calculation, writing: "Together the 12 modifiable risk factors account for around 40 percent of worldwide dementias, which consequently could theoretically be prevented or delayed." That says a lot. Imagine eliminating 40 percent of the world's dementia cases just by changing basic everyday habits.

In 2022, another study came out in the *Journal of the American Medical Association* that revealed one more modifiable risk factor to add to the list: vision impairment.[7] And this latest study's calculations are equally as breathtaking: About 100,000 current cases of dementia in the United States alone could have been prevented through healthy vision. The connection between sight and cognition may not seem so obvious, but as the authors of the study point out, our neural system maintains its function through stimulation from sensory organs, and without that stimulation, neurons will die, rearranging the brain. Eye issues are relatively easy to address with modern technologies for improving vision and clearing cataracts. And all these risk factors share crossroads. How well you see and hear, for example, affects how much you participate in activities, socialize, and generally live your life.

That said, there are 6 pillars to keep your brain sharp and reduce all these modifiable risks, which also reduces the likelihood of chronic inflammation. Let's review them in brief, as these will be your guides in carrying out the program in daily practices. If you can create daily habits that respect these pillars of brain health, you're well on your way.

THE 6 PILLARS OF YOUR BRAIN TRUST TO KEEP SHARP

PILLAR 1: NUTRITION

It's really true: You are what you eat. The link between nutrition and brain health has long been anecdotal. But now we finally have evidence to show that consuming certain foods while limiting certain other foods can help avoid memory and brain decline, protect the brain against disease, and maximize its performance. The good guys: cold-water fish, plant proteins, whole grains, extra virgin olive oil, nuts and seeds, fibrous whole fruits and vegetables—all of which typify what's called a Mediterranean-style diet that you've likely read about before. The bad guys: anything high in sugar, saturated fat, and trans-fatty acids—all of which typify the Standard American Diet, or SAD.

Eating well is more important than ever now that we know our diet can affect our brain health. The human gut microbiome—the trillions of bacteria that make their home inside our intestines—has a profound role in the health and functioning of our brains, and it turns out that what we eat contributes to the microbiome's physiology all the way up to our brains. It is a well-established gut-brain connection, with many neuroscientists referring to the intestines as our second brain.

In 2015, the MIND diet for healthy brain aging emerged, based on years of research into nutrition, aging, and Alzheimer's disease led by researchers at the Rush Institute for Healthy Aging.[8] It was created by taking two popular diets—the Mediterranean and DASH (Dietary Approaches to Stop Hypertension)—and modifying them to incorporate science-supported dietary changes that improve brain health. MIND is a catchy acronym; it stands for Mediterranean-DASH Intervention for Neurodegenerative Delay. And there's nothing surprising about the diet: thumbs-up for vegetables (especially green leafy ones), nuts, berries, beans, whole grains, fish, poultry, olive oil, and—for those interested—wine; thumbs-down on red and processed meats, butter and stick margarine, cheese, pastries and other sweets, and fried or fast food. What might surprise you is how well this diet works on the brain. In a controlled study on this way of eating over ten years of nearly a thousand people, researchers showed it could measurably prevent cognitive decline and reduce the risk of Alzheimer's disease. People who had the lowest third of MIND diet scores (meaning they followed the diet less) had the fastest rate of cognitive decline. People who had the highest third of scores experienced the slowest rate of decline. The difference between the highest third and lowest third in cognitive decline was equivalent to about seven and a half years of aging. I'll take back seven and a half years of aging, and I am sure you would as well.

People who were in the highest third of MIND diet scores had a 53 percent reduced risk of developing Alzheimer's, and those who had the middle third of scores for following the MIND diet still enjoyed a 35 percent reduction in the risk of developing the disease. Subsequent studies have further confirmed the power of this diet, including one that was published in late 2021 showing that participants in the original study who followed the MIND diet moderately did not have cognition problems later in life.[9]

While no single food is the key to good brain health, a combination of healthy foods will help insulate the brain against assault, and it is never too early to begin. Think about it. The food you eat in your youth lays the groundwork for protecting your brain in your later years. This is a point I will make repeatedly. It is never too late to start any of the lifestyle changes in the book, but that doesn't mean you should wait either. A close friend of mine just turned sixty years old. I am not exaggerating when I tell you that he is one of the healthiest, fittest people I know. Most remarkable is that he doesn't spend a lot of time exercising or even thinking about fitness. Regular movement is simply a part of his day—throughout the day. It has always been a key habit of his life, and he serves as a reminder that it is much easier to maintain something than do major repairs when it is broken. That is true when it comes to your home, your car, your body, and your brain.

You can kiss goodbye to strict dietary protocols that are unrealistic. Even though a MIND-like diet offers a framework, you'll be able to create meals that satisfy your preferences while staying on a path that fosters brain health. We're talking about a style of eating, not a rigid *eat this, not that* strong-arming directive. Food should be a source of nourishment, yes, but it should also be a source of pleasure. I go out of my dietary lane from time to time and fully savor those foods without guilt when I do. There is little space for guilt in this book, because over and over again, I heard just how bad that particular emotion is for the brain.

• • •

During the program, we will focus on the word *nourish* instead of *diet*, and aim to follow my S.H.A.R.P. protocol, which takes the best of what's been shown to be a helpful "diet" and offers an overall nutritional game plan that you can personalize:

S: Slash the Sugar and Salt, and Stick to Your ABCs. The "ABCs" is a method suggested by the Global Council on Brain Health's "Brain Food" report to discern the top-quality foods, the A-listers, from the ones we should include in moderation (B-list) or limit (C-list).[10]

H: Hydrate Smartly

A: Add More Omega-3 Fatty Acids from Dietary Sources

R: Reduce Portions

P: Plan Ahead

When people ask me about the single most important dietary hack to optimize brain function, I refer to the first letter—"S"—in the above acronym. You can't argue against the fact that all of us would do well to reduce our sugar and salt intake. It's the easiest way to gravitate toward healthier foods in general and limit the amount of processed junk.

Although precise estimates are hard to pin down, the average American consumes nearly 20 teaspoons of added sugar daily, most of that in the highly processed form of fructose, derived from high-fructose corn syrup.[11] My guess is that a lot of this sugar intake comes in the form of a liquid—soda, energy drinks, juices, flavored teas—or we eat it in processed food products, notably desserts and sweet snacks. As you will learn later in the book, sugar intake is related to brain health in a wide variety of ways, from increasing blood sugar imbalances that directly speed up cognitive decline to inducing a "type 3 diabetes" in the brain—a form of diabetes associated with Alzheimer's disease.

And while we like to think we're doing ourselves a favor by replacing refined sugar with substitutes like aspartame, saccharin, or even seminatural products like sucralose, these are not ideal. Artificial sweeteners affect gut bacteria (microbiome) in ways that lead to metabolic dysfunction, such as insulin resistance and diabetes, contributing to the same obesity epidemic for which they were marketed to solve. These are the same conditions, as you know now, that increase risk for brain decline and serious impairment. We often focus on nutrition changes to shed a few pounds or lower our cholesterol, but you will be amazed at how quickly you can emerge from brain fog and improve cognitive function with a few simple tweaks to your nourishment. That is why during Week 1 of the program, you'll be starting in your kitchen. And you won't have to evict all the sweetness from your life. There are ways to satisfy a sweet tooth with natural ingredients.

As you cut back on sugar, you'll also reduce salt intake—much of which often comes with added sugars in lots of processed foods. Salt has long been implicated in increasing the risk for high blood pressure, which in turn raises the risk of cardiovascular disease, stroke, and other health problems. But newer evidence further shows that high salt intake can activate a pathway in the brain to cause cognitive abnormalities. In other words, a high salt diet harms the brain directly. Although previous studies led researchers to think that high salt mainly caused reduced blood flow to the brain, this new research points to a high salt diet triggering a buildup of tau proteins in the brain that interfere with the proper function of brain cells, which can then lead to cognitive impairment and eventually dementia.[12] The research also has revealed that high salt adversely affects gut and immune health as well.

It can be hard to know how much salt you're consuming because so much of it hides in processed and restaurant foods.

You'll be doing yourself a favor by limiting or, ideally, nixing salty foods. And the other good news is that the research shows some of the negative affects attributed to too much salt may be reversible after twelve weeks of low-salt nutrition. If you start focusing on managing your salt intake during the first week, by the end of this program you may evade any vascular or cognitive dysfunction that could have developed from that salt intake alone. Note that the words *salt* and *sodium* are often used interchangeably. Sodium refers to a mineral—it's one of the two chemical elements found in salt, or sodium chloride, which is the crystal-like compound used in recipes and shaken on food. Sodium is the ingredient in salt that has effects on the body, and for our purposes it doesn't matter whether you call it sodium or salt. Both can damage the brain and cause cognitive deficits when there's too much.

PILLAR 2: MOVEMENT (NOT JUST "EXERCISE")

This should not come as a surprise. Movement, both aerobic and anaerobic (strength training), is not only good for the body; it's even better for the brain. Think of it as the brain's only superfood! Physical exertion, in fact, has thus far been the only thing we've scientifically documented to improve brain health and function. While we can record associations between, say, eating healthier foods and having a healthier brain, the connection between physical fitness and brain fitness is clear, direct, and powerful. Movement can increase your brainpower by helping to increase, repair, and maintain brain cells, and it makes you more productive and more alert throughout the day.

I make an effort to use the word *movement* rather than *exercise* because it exudes a more positive vibe and lacks the implication of being a dreaded chore. Movement also entails more than formal exercise or push-ups—it is vital to life. Perhaps most importantly, movement is one of the most reliable ways to release a protein substance known as BDNF, or brain-derived neurotrophic factor.[13] One prominent neuroscientist described it as "Miracle-Gro" for your brain.[14] In addition to nurturing the birth of new brain cells (neurogenesis), BDNF also helps protect existing neurons, ensuring their survival while encouraging synapse formation, the connection of one neuron to another. Interestingly, studies have demonstrated decreased levels of BDNF in Alzheimer's patients.[15] No surprise then that scientists are looking for ways to increase BDNF in the brain through basic lifestyle habits. At the top of their list: movement.

This is one area where the adage "what is good for the heart is good for the brain" doesn't hold up neatly. While more intense aerobic activity is better for the heart, moderate activity such as brisk walking appears better for the brain. Scientists have speculated that BDNF is released in both situations, but the excess cortisol secreted with intense activity—especially when that intensity is prolonged—inhibits BDNF function.[16] For your heart, go for a run, but for your brain, slow the pace down to a brisk walk. Ideally, you should plan on engaging in moderate activities daily that are just intense enough to raise your heart rate and pump more nourishing blood throughout the body (and brain). Then at intervals throughout the week, plan to incorporate strength training to support bone and muscle health. More muscle mass also means more blood flow to the brain, as well as more BDNF production. There is plenty of evidence that you will naturally get some cardio and muscle training through everyday activities such as walking, lifting objects, and using stairs, but you should still make an extra effort to amplify both cardiac output and muscle use. You don't have to get on a "dreadmill" or lift weights every day, but you do need to think about ways to increase your heart rate daily and perform some muscle training two to three days a week on nonconsecutive days. I won't give you strict guidelines here, but I will be asking you to document your "exercise" during the program. By documenting your workouts and assessing how you feel, you can then make modifications to arrive at an ideal routine *for you.*

Movement is the single most important thing you can do *over-all* to enhance your brain's function and resilience against disease. Fitness could very well be the most important ingredient to living as long as possible, despite all the other risk factors you bear, including age and genetics. And while it may seem hard to believe, I must reiterate that regular movement is the only behavioral activity scientifically proven to trigger biological effects that can help the brain. We cannot yet say that movement will reverse cognitive deficits and dementia, but evidence is mounting to get in motion. Exercise may slow memory loss, and new research shows that exercise can reverse cognitive decline in aging mice, which is paving the way for human studies.[17] Remember: A body in motion tends to stay in motion. And, if you have not been moving and breaking a sweat regularly, starting today can significantly protect your brain later. Again, it's never too late, or too early! Physical movement may offer the greatest return on investment in yourself, and it's an antidote to many things that play into your risk for decline.

DON'T UNDERESTIMATE THE POWER OF MUSCLE MASS

When people think about "exercise," their minds often gravitate toward activities that mainly work the cardiovascular system. But don't forget about building and preserving muscle mass, one of the body's unsung heroes. Loss of muscle tissue, in fact, contributes significantly to physical decline that in turn impacts the brain. Studies are underway to show the link between physical muscle health and brain health, but so far the evidence is clear: Low muscle mass is associated with steeper cognitive decline and greater risk of dementia.[18]

Aging involves a gradual, natural muscle loss over time that speeds up as one gets older unless you're making a concerted effort to support that muscle mass and strength. And there's a relationship between the state of your muscle mass and length of life. The progressive loss of muscle mass and function that typically occurs with aging is called sarcopenia, and it can impact your ability to perform basic daily tasks, ultimately eroding your quality of life over time. Put simply, muscle mass and strength are key to survival and losing them is not inevitable.

In 2021, the Centers for Disease Control and Prevention released a large study finding that cognitive decline is almost twice as common among adults who are inactive compared to those who are active.[19] And shockingly, the study highlighted that an estimated 11.2 percent of U.S. adults who are forty-five years old or older have what's called subjective cognitive decline, which is the experience of worsening or more frequent confusion or memory loss within the previous year. The prevalence of that subjective cognitive decline increased as physical activity level decreased. So, the lesson is clear: Move more and move often. Don't find yourself sitting for more than an hour without getting up and moving around.

A few years ago, I visited an indigenous people deep in the middle of the Amazon rain forest called the Tsimane. I was interested in them because they were thought to have the healthiest hearts in the world. When I was there, researchers also shared new data showing this same people had hardly any evidence of diabetes or dementia, and the researchers thought a big factor was their constant movement. The only people I ever saw sitting were the oldest members of the group. Most of the Tsimane were either standing and walking during the daylight hours (though of course they will gather around a shared meal sitting down) or lying flat at night. I rarely saw the Tsimane run. Even when they were hunting, they briskly walked and tracked their prey until the animal got tired, which is when they went in for the kill. The average number of daily steps was around 17,000—a lot but also very doable. For the Tsimane, consistent moderate movement appeared to offer a lot of benefit, something we could incorporate into our daily lives as well. Just keep moving, remembering that inactivity is the culprit for so many diseases. Too much sitting sinks your body—and your brain.

Not all of us can engage in nonstop activity all day. Getting up for light activity such as walking for two minutes every hour has been shown to be associated with a 33 percent lower chance of dying over a three-year period.[20] Two minutes! That's a big boost in prevention for a short period of time. A mere 120 seconds each hour can offset the damaging effects that prolonged sitting has on the body.

THE MAGIC OF MOVEMENT

Regular movement that increases blood flow and works your muscles has long been linked to brain health. A big factor is the control of blood sugar through that motion. Using sugar to fuel your muscles helps prevent dramatic glucose and insulin fluctuations that increase the risk for dementia. Consistent moderate-intensity movement also helps lower inflammation and that is critical in preventing dementia. Consider these other benefits:

- Lowered risk of death from all causes
- Increased stamina, strength, flexibility, and energy
- Increased muscle tone and bone health
- Increased blood and lymph circulation and oxygen supply to cells and tissues
- More restful sleep
- Stress reduction
- Increased self-esteem, confidence, and sense of well-being
- Release of endorphins, the brain chemicals that act as natural mood lifters and pain relievers
- Decreased blood sugar levels and risk for insulin resistance and diabetes
- Ideal weight distribution and smaller waist circumference
- Increased heart health, with lower risk for cardiovascular disease and high blood pressure
- Decreased inflammation and risk for age-related disease, from cancer to dementia
- Stronger immune system

Adequate, brain-boosting movement includes a combination of purposeful aerobic cardio work (e.g., swimming, cycling, jogging, group cardio classes, playing tennis or pickleball); strength training (free weights, resistance bands, gym machines, mat Pilates, lunges, squats); and routines that promote flexibility, and coordination and balance (stretching, yoga). But don't think in terms of just exercise. Movement also includes leading a physically active life throughout the day—taking the stairs instead of the elevator; avoiding prolonged sitting; going for walks during breaks; performing household chores; engaging in hobbies such as dancing, hiking, and gardening.

If you're not already moving enough, you'll get going in Week 2. For me, regular movement is a daily nonnegotiable ritual like brushing my teeth. It'll be the same for you.

PILLAR 3: DOWNTIME (IN WAKING HOURS)

It's not stress that kills us, it's our reaction to it.

—Hans Selye

Dr. Hans Selye is credited with coining *stress* as it is used today. Selye is regarded as one of the founding fathers of stress research. In 1936 he defined stress as "the non-specific response of the body to any demand for change." His work followed that of his predecessor, Dr. Walter Bradford Cannon, who was chairman of the department of physiology at Harvard Medical School and introduced the term "fight or flight" to describe an animal's response to threats. Prescient as he was, Selye proposed that when subjected to persistent stress, both humans and animals could develop certain life-threatening afflictions such as heart attacks or strokes that previously were thought to be caused only by specific pathogens.

It was a revolutionary idea at the time, but one we've come to appreciate as fact with plenty of scientific evidence collected through the past century that shows the impact that everyday life and experiences have not only on our emotional well-being but also on our physical health. Interestingly, the word *stress* as it relates to emotions didn't become part of our everyday vocabulary until the 1950s. Then its use became even more common with the onset of the Cold War, which was an era riddled with fear, and we favored the word *stress* to describe feeling afraid of atomic war. Today we continue to use the word to describe anything that disrupts us emotionally, whether it's the threat of global war or disagreements in our relationships and tough situations at work.

On a scale of 1 to 10, 10 being the most extreme, how would you rate your stress level? What if I told you that stress is now considered a trigger for silent neurodegeneration, which occurs years before any symptoms develop? Look, the goal of living a stress-free life is neither realistic nor worthy. Truth is, we need stress. It's what helps us get out of bed in the morning, study for an exam, and feel motivated to try new things. Stress is not the enemy, but relentless stress is a big driver of the worst health crises in the wealthiest countries, including poor mental health. In Robert Sapolsky's seminal book *Why Zebras Don't Get Ulcers,* he makes the point that a zebra being chased has stress levels off the charts, but as soon as it is free, the zebra is happily grazing, stress-free. We humans need to live more like zebras.

The third pillar—downtime—encompasses many things, from finding ways to turn the volume down on your psychological stress to ensuring you're giving your brain the physical recesses it needs to regroup and recuperate itself.[21] And I'm talking about breaks in your waking hours during which you engage in an activity that's peaceful, meditative, and stress-reducing.

Relaxing, or making space for downtime, is not solely a biological thing for the body; your brain needs to chill out too. Scores of well-designed studies routinely show that chronic stress can impair your ability to learn and adapt to new situations and subtly erode your cognition. More specifically, stress destroys cells in the hippocampus, the brain site responsible for memory storage and retrieval. So, by reducing stress you not only help preserve cells vital to memory but you also improve focus, concentration, and productivity. Less stress also gives you more peace of mind. And we can't ignore that stress also feeds into levels of anxiety and overall mood, which in turn affect risk for depression while promoting inflammation.

There's no shortage of ways to lower the volume on your stress levels. Ideas abound: deep breathing exercises; restorative yoga classes (or merely ten minutes of refreshing stretching); leisure walks in nature (nature therapy); journal writing; light reading; listening to music; practicing mindfulness through meditation; talking to a good friend; spending time with a pet; and even daydreaming. You'll use the program to find what works for you and schedule more downtime into your days, no matter how hectic they are. Some downtime activities, like going to the spa, will demand more planning, but little everyday moments of downtime are just as important and require some intention. For you, maybe setting an alarm on your phone for a dedicated time each day when you call a time-out to do something relaxing would work magic in minutes.

I have always found it remarkable how quickly some of these techniques work. Calming yourself down takes a mere ninety seconds with simple breathing exercises that settle your nervous system. When you are stressed, your body's sympathetic nervous system is activated. That is the fight-or-flight response that raises your blood pressure, constricts your blood vessels, and gives you that pit in your stomach. It's like hitting the gas pedal in the car. The parasympathetic nervous system is the opposite, the rest and digest system. It allows your body to relax, open up airways, and even improves your emotional health. Here is the good news: A few deep abdominal breaths from your diaphragm can quickly change your physiology and tip the scales toward your parasympathetic response. Because it is so easy, people often dismiss the incredible power of deep focused breaths. But now that you know what the parasympathetic nervous system is, and how to control it, you are likely to engage in this behavior and hopefully encourage your loved ones to do the same.

I hope you try at least one breathing exercise and find a collection of strategies in the program to incorporate into your life right away. Stress will always be there, but it doesn't have to always affect you negatively. How you respond to that stress—and lighten your stress load overall—is what matters most.

PILLAR 4: RESTORATIVE SLEEP

Even a soul submerged in sleep is hard at work
and helps make something of the world.

—Heraclitus

Sleep—of course—is the ultimate rest. Poor sleep can lead to impaired memory and over time increase risk for serious brain decline and disease.[22] Two thirds of us who live in the modern, developed world are chronically sleep-deprived. That's tens of millions of us.

Chronic inadequate sleep puts us at higher risk for dementia, depression and mood disorders, learning and memory problems, heart disease, high blood pressure, weight gain and obesity, diabetes, fall-related injuries, immune dysfunction, and cancer. It can even spark biases in behavior, causing us to focus on negative information when making decisions. Sleep is essential for consolidating our memories and filing them away for later recall. Research shows that brief bursts of brain activity during deep sleep, called sleep spindles, effectively move recent memories, including what we learned that day, from the short-term space of the hippocampus to the "hard drive" of our neocortex.[23] Sleep, in other words, cleans up the hippocampus so it can take in new information that it then processes. Without sleep, this memory organization cannot happen.

More than just affecting memory, a sleep deficit prevents you from processing information. So not only do you lack the ability to remember, you cannot even interpret information—to take in and think about it. Among the more recent and captivating findings about sleep has been discovering its "washing" effects on the brain.[24] The body clears waste and fluid from tissues through the lymphatic system, which goes into overdrive during sleep. The brain has a "clean cycle" system for washing away metabolic debris and junk, including sticky proteins that can contribute to those amyloid plaques in diseased brains. Sleep is the button that turns on the clean cycle process. In fact, the electrical signals in the brain that fire during slow wave sleep are what help set the rinse cycle in motion. If you're not getting enough sleep to capture slow wave sleep, which is the deepest phase of non-rapid eye movement (NREM) sleep (also called deep sleep), then you're not clearing out that waste as well. In 2019, researchers recorded the waves of electrical activity that were followed by waves of cerebrospinal fluid circulating through the brain.[25]

Lack of sleep is not something to celebrate—or even boast

about. If you think rising at 4:00 a.m. after going to bed at midnight will make you more successful, think again. There is no data that shows successful people get less sleep, despite the trend among celebrities and entrepreneurs to extol the virtues of their late nights followed by super-early mornings. My hope is that you begin to prioritize sleep; it will be a key element of the program alongside strategies to reduce stress. We all need seven to nine hours nightly, and yet on average, Americans sleep fewer than seven hours a night—about two fewer hours than they did a century ago.

Dr. Matthew Walker, a professor of neuroscience and psychology at the University of California, Berkeley, is among today's pioneering researchers in sleep.[26] He used to say that sleep is the third pillar of good health, alongside nourishment and movement. But given his latest finding about how sleep supports the brain and nervous system, he now teaches that sleep is the single most effective thing we can do to reset our brains and bodies, as well as increase a healthy life span. How could something we spend about twenty-five years of our lives doing be useless?

Contrary to popular belief, sleep is not a state of neural idleness. It is a critical phase during which the body replenishes itself in a variety of ways that ultimately affect every system, from the brain to the heart, the immune system, and all the inner workings of our metabolism. It is normal for sleep to change with age, but poor-quality sleep with age is not normal. While sleep disorders such as sleep apnea and early waking become more common with age, they can often be treated with simple lifestyle changes.

This program will help you reclaim your right to a good night's sleep—and achieve it on a regular basis.

PILLAR 5: DISCOVERY

For each additional year you keep working, the risk of getting dementia is reduced by 3.2 percent.[27] Read that sentence again. It is the continued work that is protective here, not dozing off on a beach. Now, 3.2 percent might not seem like much of a reduction in risk, but in real life it's huge. The study behind this finding included nearly half a million people, showing that someone who retired at age sixty-five had about a 15 percent lower risk of developing dementia compared to someone retiring at sixty, even after other factors were taken into account. Staying engaged in a job, especially one that's satisfying, tends to keep people not just mentally challenged and socially connected but also more physically active—all things known to protect cognition. Takeaway: Retire late, or never at all. (Queen Elizabeth II worked until her death at ninety-six!)

This surprises a lot of people who imagine they'll be more physically active when they are no longer working, but the opposite is true. If you stay employed longer, you are more likely to also stay physically active.

The science behind this astonishing fact? Work builds and sustains your cognitive reserve by making demands on your brain that keeps it thinking, strategizing, learning, and solving problems. Cognitive reserve is a reflection of how much you have challenged your brain over the years through your education, work, and other activities. Epidemiologic evidence suggests that people with higher IQ, education, occupational achievements, who participate in leisure activities such as hobbies or sports have a reduced risk of developing Alzheimer's disease. These pursuits force the brain to continually acquire knowledge and work with it in ways that ultimately build new networks and strengthen existing ones. Not surprisingly, animal studies show that cognitive stimulation increases the density of neurons, synapses, and dendrites. Put more simply, cognitive stimulation builds a brain more resistant to disease, such as dementia.

Stimulating your brain doesn't only mean working at a job for a living. Volunteering and engaging in your community and with friends and family can stimulate your brain too. It is both the ongoing discovery that occurs with continually challenging your brain, usually through a purposeful activity, that seems to be the key to bolstering your brain health as you age.[28]

In 2022, researchers at University College London announced that a sense of purpose was associated with a 19 percent reduced rate of clinically significant cognitive impairment.[29] And a mentally stimulating job could postpone the onset of dementia by 1.5 years.

Unfortunately, most people get it wrong when it comes to defining cognitively stimulating activities that facilitate new discoveries. Although there's a time and place for challenging the mind with games and puzzles or online video games, don't let those activities distract you from engaging in the kinds of pursuits that are truly cognitively stimulating: picking up a new hobby, like painting or digital photography, or even learning a new piece of software or language. Having a sense of purpose will also help keep your brain plastic and preserve that cognitive reserve. With purpose comes a love for life and all the experiences it offers. Purpose also puts a damper on depression, which can be common in one's later years and is a huge risk factor in itself for memory decline, stroke, and dementia.

Lead a rich, active, dynamic, complex life.

—Dr. Adam Gazzaley, professor of neurology, physiology, and psychiatry, University of California, San Francisco

PILLAR 6: CONNECTION

Let us be grateful to people who make us happy; they are the charming gardeners who make our souls blossom.

—Marcel Proust

We tend to underestimate the value of our friendships and romantic partnerships to our health. But they are key to wellness and preventing cognitive decline. Big-time. Social contact enhances cognitive reserve and encourages beneficial behaviors. Several studies of thousands of people over the course of decades have shown that those who enjoy more frequent social contact at midlife are least likely to develop dementia later on. We are social creatures who need social connection to thrive, especially when it comes to brain health. A look at the data shows that enjoying close ties to friends and family, as well as participating in meaningful social activities, may help keep your mind sharp and your memories strong. And it's not just the number of social connections you have. The type, quality, and purpose of your relationships can affect your brain functions as well.

During the pandemic, I learned a valuable insight from a loneliness researcher, Dr. Stephanie Cacioppo of the University of Chicago. On my podcast, I told her that I am incredibly close to my parents, but when we had spoken on the phone lately, our conversations had become trivial. "Fine," was always the answer I would get when calling to check in on them. Cacioppo suggested I do something unusual the next time I spoke with them: Ask for help. It didn't need to be some big request, but even something relatively simple. My parents are both automotive engineers so I decided to ask them about some smoke I had seen coming from under the hood of my car. They were immediately engaged, reading glasses on, asking me to pop the hood and show them on FaceTime. The next day they called again with another diagnosis for the problem. This small beginning led to deeper conversations about unrelated topics. Such an easy strategy can apply to any relationship, not just familial ones. Maybe the lesson is obvious, but everyone desires some sense of purpose in a relationship, and this was an easy and authentic way to create it.

The second lesson is that our most profound relationships are often with people with whom we can be vulnerable, flawed, and at times, in need of help. Asking my parents for help, even though I am a grown man in his fifties, was a simple way to show my vulnerability and deepen our relationship in the process. Over and over again, you will hear it's not the quantity of relationships that matters as much as the quality, and this is one strategy to improve the quality.

The evidence is increasingly clear that staying social and interacting with others in meaningful ways can provide a buffer against the harmful effects of stress on the brain.[30] I see the anecdotal evidence of this every day in my work as a neurosurgeon and out in the field as a journalist. The people I meet who are the liveliest and most joyful despite their advanced age are the ones who maintain high-quality friendships, loving families, and an expansive, dynamic social network.

The problem is that social isolation and feelings of loneliness are on the rise in our society. It's the paradox of our era: We
are hyperconnected through technology yet increasingly drifting
apart from each other and suffering from loneliness because we
lack authentic connection. This absence of real connection is of
epidemic proportions, and we're suffering dire physical, mental,
and emotional consequences, especially among older adults, with
about one third of Americans older than sixty-five, and half of
those over eighty-five, now living alone.

People with fewer meaningful social connections have disrupted
sleep patterns, altered immune systems, more inflammation, and
higher levels of stress hormones. Isolation has been found to increase the risk of heart disease by 29 percent and stroke by 32
percent; loneliness has been shown to accelerate cognitive decline
in older adults.[31] In a study involving 3.4 million people, individuals who were mostly on their own had a 30 percent higher risk of
dying in the next seven years, and surprise: This effect was largest
in people younger than sixty-five![32] Data like this speaks to me. It
tells me to pay attention to my relationships as much as I do to
my health through diet and exercise. High-quality socialization is
akin to a vital sign.

For most of my life, I have never been the quintessential social
person. Some have described me as socially awkward, but I don't
think that was the issue as much as my previous inability to see
the value of being social. I enjoyed it, but mostly saw social time
as a luxury or a frivolity, especially since I was busy studying to
become a neurosurgeon. During the pandemic, though, I completely changed my mind on this. Granted, I had plenty of enter-
tainment at home between my wife and three teenage daughters,
but something was missing from the picture, as many of us experienced in lockdown. When I was unable to spend time with

friends and extended family, I really missed it, at a visceral level. I could tell that something was off not just in how I felt but also with my thinking. I felt my empathy starting to shrink, and my outlook becoming increasingly grim. At times I felt as if I was in a daze, missing a full, rich context to life from people around me other than my immediate family. As soon as I got together with a few friends one evening safely outdoors, it was like a salve for my brain. I felt happier, more connected, full of empathy, and, yes, sharper. I even shocked my wife when I suggested we call the neighbors over for dinner one recent evening. I relished their company, but now also know that I am tangibly investing in my brain health.

And if you need any more convincing, then I invite you to check out Dr. Robert Waldinger's popular TED talk on the subject of relationships ("What Makes a Good Life?"), which has been viewed tens of millions of times. A psychiatrist at Massachusetts General Hospital and a professor of psychiatry at Harvard Medical School, Dr. Waldinger directs the Harvard Study of Adult Development, which tracks how health is influenced by connections between people.[33] It's become the world's longest scientific study on happiness ever conducted. Turns out whether we have people around us we can rely on determines a lot of our happiness and cognitive function. The strength of our connections with others can *predict* the health of both our bodies and our brains as we go through life. Good relationships protect us. Period.

So, in this program, you're going to work on your relationships as much as your physical health. Get ready to talk to strangers and expand your social network. You don't need to be married or in a committed relationship to benefit. This is about all your connections, from casual friendships to family members, coworkers, classmates, sports partners, study groups, neighbors, even casual acquaintances and people who provide services for you like the appliance repairman or delivery person. Prepare to deepen your connections—they are the secret sauce to a long, sharp life.

> *Live in rooms full of light. Avoid heavy food. Be moderate in drinking wine. Take massages, baths, exercise and gymnastics. Fight insomnia with gentle rocking or the sound of running water. Change surroundings and take long journeys. Strictly avoid frightening ideas. Indulge in cheerful conversation and amusements. Listen to music.*
>
> —*De Medicina*, Aulus Cornelius Celsus, c. 25 BCE–50 CE

GET YOUR GAME ON AND PREPARE FOR THE ROAD AHEAD

COMMITMENT

Step one is commitment. You've already committed just by picking up this book, but you might need an extra push. Think about what you want to get out of this program beyond a better brain. Mark all that apply on the following "Commitment Questionnaire":

COMMITMENT QUESTIONNAIRE

- ☐ More energy
- ☐ More productivity
- ☐ More confidence and self-esteem
- ☐ Deeper relationships
- ☐ Less weight
- ☐ Greater sense of joy and optimism
- ☐ More youthful appearance
- ☐ Relief from and prevention of chronic conditions

❏ Fewer aches and pains

❏ Less anxiety, worry, and feelings of depression

❏ Stronger resilience to stressors

❏ Sounder sleep

❏ Physical fitness and body positivity (feeling good about your body)

❏ Heightened immunity

❏ A feeling of more control in your life

❏ More time to do whatever you want (have more fun!)

I hope you marked just about all those boxes! They are all achievable with your commitment to the program. A reminder that I am only trying to share the wisdom I have humbly gained but that I am confident can probably improve your brain health. Again, most of us have never even tried to improve our brain, believing it wasn't possible. That is why even small changes will have so much impact. And that last one about time may seem counterintuitive, but once you've set yourself up for optimal brain health, guess what: Everything else in life flows more efficiently and you won't waste time. In other words, focus on your brain and everything else will follow.

The brain is ground zero. It is what makes you *you*. Your heart ticks, yes, but it's your brain that ultimately makes you tick and determines your quality of life and how you perceive everything around you. Without a healthy brain, you cannot make healthy decisions (or you'll spend too much time trying to make them). And with a healthy brain comes not only a healthy body, weight, heart, and so on, but also a stronger sense of confidence, a more solid financial future thanks to smarter decisions, better relationships, more love and laughter in your life, and heightened overall happiness.

Now let's obliterate a few excuses you might have:

- *I don't have the time.* Yes, you do. Everyone is time-starved, but we all prioritize what's important and this program should be no less valuable to your well-being than brushing your teeth (and flossing!). Anything worth accomplishing takes patience, perseverance, and incremental effort, especially when the goals are worthy ones with incredible returns on your investment of time.

- *I don't think I have it in me to complete this program—it's intimidating.* Think progress, not perfection. All the little shifts you make will add up to large changes overall. Your success accumulates. Readers have told me the program made them feel like their brain was running for the first time, when it had only previously crawled. That should be inspiring enough. Also, it is critical to remember that self-care should not be an on-and-off proposition. Don't be like those who fall into the trap of repeatedly neglecting themselves. And when you need to find consistency in your routines and new habits, don't get complacent—continue to find important motivators. Motivators can be anything from an upcoming family vacation to running a 10K or perhaps a medical scare in your family that made you think about your own health. Your motivators will help you push past low points and remind you why you have decided to make these changes. Have faith in your power of change. I'll be giving you room to write down how you're feeling along the way and help you process any negative emotions. A healthy brain doesn't mean you won't have bad days; it means you are far less likely to be crushed by them. A healthy brain will seek challenges and difficulty, realizing those experiences strengthen the brain like a muscle. The point is your mental attitude has a lot to do with your success. If you feel "ruined" by a day and fall off the proverbial wagon, don't give up. Tomorrow is always a new day. By having a record of your difficult days on paper, you'll more easily identify behavioral patterns, pitfalls, and roadblocks that prevent you from making the most of the program and adopting this brain-friendly lifestyle. Approach the program as a series of fun challenges rather than chores to check off. And think about how you'll feel after—clearer-minded, leaner, more loving and accepting of yourself, more the person you want to be. The payoffs are huge here. Don't lose sight of them.

- *I know there will be aspects of the program I won't be able to do or sustain for long.* I've designed this program to be as adaptable as possible; after all, there are nearly eight billion unique brains on the planet. Think of this more like a menu. One of the purposes of this program is to help you tailor all the best science-based strategies that support brain health to your own life and preferences. You'll find plenty of alternatives if you encounter a recommendation or challenge you don't want to do. The important thing is that you don't allow any obstacle to prevent you from moving forward. If you skip over a challenge, that's perfectly fine. Just make note of it and aim to make up for it later or in some other way that works for you. This program is not meant to be rigid and followed to the T. As already noted, go at your own pace, respect the needs of your body, and surrender to the process. From the moment you begin to make small changes in how you live—what you eat, how much you move, and so on—your body will undergo a multitude of invisible changes, all of which build and set a strong foundation for dramatic results in the future. Do your best with what you've got every day, and things will work out.

- *I've never put myself first like this before. I have too many other demands. I'll fail or at least drive my family members crazy.* I don't know anyone who doesn't feel a little guilty when they decide to put themselves above others, including loved ones. But if you don't prioritize yourself, you won't be able to show up in life—for yourself and your beloveds—as best you can or at all. We tell passengers on planes to put their oxygen masks on first before others for a reason—it increases the chances of survival for all on board. But I understand the dilemma. Between work deadlines, household chores, raising children, and perhaps helping older family members, it's a bit reflexive to cater to everyone and everything else first. I get it. We're busy and the expectations on us are high. But without your health and optimal brain function, what will you have? How can you help anyone else live up to their full potential without working on your own? When your brain is healthy, you will feel more present and people will take notice. You will be less frazzled, more in control, and able to contribute substantially, both at work and at play. People who sacrifice their own needs for everyone else are likely doomed to eventually burn out and experience a brain bust. Then everyone loses. Give yourself the gift of this program. You deserve it. Enlist family members to support you or even join you on this journey. If you make it a team effort, you stack the deck in favor of your success. Schedule this program into your life as you would anything else vital. And schedule it again and again until these lessons and their activities are second nature.

> *You may have to fight a battle more than once to win it.*
> —Margaret Thatcher

WHAT'S STOPPING YOU?

What barriers might prevent you from committing to this program? Even without knowing the specifics of the program yet, you might have some hesitations about changing your current lifestyle and daily habits. Write down what might get in your way of proceeding:

_____

_____

_____

MAKE THE COMMITMENT

The bigger question you need to ask yourself at this point is whether you are ready. If yes, then take the following oath by repeating these statements:

- I will take my health seriously and modify my eating and other behaviors for life.

- I will make an effort to prioritize myself and the habits that either help or hinder my well-being.

- I will accept the fact that this isn't just about looking or feeling better—it's about making a change in my life that will positively affect every aspect of who I am, from a spiritual, emotional, cognitive, and physical standpoint.

- I will use these next 12 weeks to set the stage for a sharper brain for life!

SELF-ASSESSMENT: WHERE ARE YOU IN YOUR QUEST TO OPTIMIZE BRAIN HEALTH AND AVOID DECLINE?

Before beginning any journey, especially one that aims to elevate your brain health, it helps to have an idea of where you are now—and where there's room for improvement. I like data, especially when it comes to an honest assessment of your current brain health. Circle Yes, No, or I Don't Know to the following fifteen straightforward questions. If you find yourself on the fence between a solid Yes or No, go with "I Don't Know" (which can mean you're not sure, or you feel like you're sometimes a strong Yes but other times a No). If it helps, you can also interpret the Yes as "True," the No as "False," and the I Don't Know as sometimes "True" and sometimes "False."

Be sincere and forthright with yourself. Nobody will see your responses unless you choose to share them. These questions are going to elicit and quantify your risk factors for brain decline. The questions are data-driven insofar as they reflect scientific findings to date. But don't panic if you find yourself answering No a lot. Remember, it's never too late to start. If your current habits are not brain-healthy, it only means you have even more to gain from this guide. The whole point of this workbook is to get you on the right path. The more you're aware of your habits, the more you're able to make the changes that will positively impact your brain's life and health.

It is always striking how much people over- or underestimate their behaviors. Only when they are forced to really evaluate and quantify their lifestyle do they become aware of their weaknesses and strengths. This test will arm you with crucial personal data that will ultimately provide guidance for where you should be putting more effort—to rebuild and maintain a better brain. After the quiz, I encourage you to write down the top three areas in your life where you may want to devote the most attention during the 12-week program. Most of these risk factors are modifiable (and I've intentionally left out risk factors you cannot control such as your genetics, gender, or age). Remember: Regardless of your heritage or age, you have the power to change the trajectory of your brain health starting today.

1 I enjoy a lively, satisfying social life with a close-knit group of friends and family members.

YES | NO | I DON'T KNOW

2 I keep a regular fitness routine that challenges me physically, gets my heart rate up, and makes me go a little breathless sometimes.

YES | NO | I DON'T KNOW

3 I move a lot throughout the day and don't sit for long periods of time.

YES | NO | I DON'T KNOW

4 I am at a healthy weight.

YES | NO | I DON'T KNOW

5 I do not have any cardiovascular or metabolic conditions (e.g., high blood pressure, insulin resistance, diabetes, high cholesterol).

YES | NO | I DON'T KNOW

6 I have not been diagnosed with an infection that can lead to chronic inflammation and can have neurological effects (e.g., Lyme disease, herpes, syphilis, long Covid).

YES | NO | I DON'T KNOW

7 I do not take any medications with known possible brain effects (e.g., antidepressants, antianxiety drugs, blood pressure drugs, statins, proton pump inhibitors, antihistamines).

YES | NO | I DON'T KNOW

8 I have not experienced a traumatic brain injury or suffered head trauma from an accident or playing an impact sport.

YES | NO | I DON'T KNOW

9 I do not have a history of depression.

YES | NO | I DON'T KNOW

10 I do not have a history of smoking or alcohol abuse.

YES | NO | I DON'T KNOW

11   I regularly sleep well, banking seven to nine hours a night, and feel refreshed most mornings.

YES | NO | I DON'T KNOW

12   I'm cognitively challenged daily with my activities and engagements with others (work and play).

YES | NO | I DON'T KNOW

13   I feel like my life has a purpose, I enjoy learning new things, and I make an effort to try new endeavors.

YES | NO | I DON'T KNOW

14   I maintain a diet low in processed foods, sugars, and salt, and I eat whole grains, fish, nuts, olive oil, and fresh fruits and vegetables.

YES | NO | I DON'T KNOW

15   I cope well with stress and make efforts to manage it; I don't feel like I live with chronic, unrelenting stress that subverts the quality of my life.

YES | NO | I DON'T KNOW

Scoring: For every circled No, give yourself a point. For every I Don't Know, give yourself half a point. Yes answers get no points. Tally up your score. This is like a game of golf: You want the lowest score possible.

0–5 = Bravo. You're in the minority of people who are ahead of the game and following a lifestyle playbook that helps prevent cognitive decline. You'll still likely want to keep fine-tuning your habits and continue to improve. Keep going!

6–10 = You probably have good days and bad days with living a lifestyle that supports brain health. But you're on your way. Keep working on your weak spots and push your tally number down.

11–15 = It's time to rethink and reset your lifestyle and build a new foundation for building a better brain. You can do this, and remember that you should think of yourself having the most to gain, not the least. Highlight the responses that surprised you the most. Keep those risk factors at the forefront of your focus during the program.

My Three Biggest Weak Spots (example: poor sleep, not enough exercise, too much sugar):

1 _____

2 _____

3 _____

GOALS

My hunch is you've got a few goals swirling around in your head right now. Let's set some here in writing. Pick three goals to articulate across three categories—physical, mental/emotional, and general life. By "general life," I'm referring to life goals that could relate to your work, your relationships, or your personal pursuits and dreams. Be as specific and detailed as possible.

Physical:

_____

_____

_____

Mental/emotional:

_____

_____

_____

General life:

_____

_____

_____

Who can support you on your journey? Who can help hold you accountable? Name that person here and let them know your intentions for this program:

_____

_____

READY,
SET,
GO . . .

Think of this as a master class on how to build a better brain, which opens the door to whatever you want to get out of life—including being a better parent, child, friend, or partner. You can be more creative and fulfilled, as well as more available for everyone you love. You will also develop more resilience so you aren't derailed by the trials of daily life. These goals are all far more connected than you may realize.

Believing you can always be better tomorrow is an audacious way to view the world, and one that has shaped my own life. Since I was a teenager, I've always worked hard on my physical health—to make my body stronger, faster, and more robust against illness and injury. I think everyone has different motivations for taking care of their own health. For many, it is to feel better, achieve more, and to be there for their children or other family members. For others, it is about attaining a certain physical appearance or to participate in a race or sporting event.

Whatever the reason though, I cannot reiterate this enough: Once your brain is running cleanly and smoothly, a number of positive outcomes will stem from that sharper brain. There are even studies showing that your pain tolerance increases, your need for medications decreases, and your ability to heal strengthens. Nearly every doctor I have spoken to about this subject has said some variation of the following: To best take care of your body, you have to first take care of your mind. It is true, and the best part is that it is not that hard to do. Think of it as periodic little tweaks and adjustments instead of wholesale changes in your life.

As you go through this workbook, I don't want you to be running away scared from something. The fear of dementia should not be the motivation for you to read this book. Instead, I want you to be running enthusiastically toward something—running toward knowledge that can keep your brain in peak shape and withstand the test of your time on this planet. This is a "top-down" project.

THE DIRTY DOZEN: MYTHS TO DITCH

Myth #1: The Brain Remains a Complete Mystery

False. There's a lot more we know about the brain today and how to keep it sharp longer.

Myth #2: Older People Are Doomed to Forget Things

False. Some cognitive skills do decline as you age but memory falters because you are not paying close attention.

Myth #3: Dementia Is an Inevitable Consequence of Old Age

False. Age-related changes in the brain are not the same as changes that are caused by disease, and the former can be slowed to decrease the risk of the latter.

Myth #4: Older People Can't Learn New Things

False! Learning can happen at any age, especially when you also participate in cognitively stimulating activities like meeting new people or trying new hobbies.

Myth #5: You Must Master One Language Before Learning Another

False. Different areas of the brain do not battle; children learn a new language more easily than adults mostly because they are less self-conscious. But anyone at any age can pick up a new language.

Myth #6: A Person Who Has Memory Training Never Forgets

False. "Use it or lose it" applies to memory training in the same way it applies to maintaining the strength of a muscle or your overall physical health. In other words, you need to keep working your brain in ways that strengthen its networks just as you need to work your muscles to keep them strong.

Myth #7: We Use Only 10 Percent of Our Brains

False. Experiments using brain scans show that much of the brain is engaged even during simple tasks, and injury to the small sections of the brain called "eloquent areas" can have profound consequences for language, movement, emotion, or sensory perception.

Myth #8: Male and Female Brains Differ in Ways That Dictate Learning Abilities and Intelligence

False. Differences do exist in the brains of males and females that result in variations in brain function, but not to the extent that one is better "equipped" than the other; no research has ever demonstrated gender-specific distinctions in how neural networks connect when we learn new skills.

Myth #9: A Crossword Puzzle a Day Can Keep the Brain Doctor Away

Not necessarily. Crossword puzzles flex only a portion of your brain so they won't keep your brain sharp without additional exercises.

Myth #10: You Are Dominated by Either Your "Right" or "Left" Brain

False. Brain-scanning technology has revealed that the brain's two hemispheres most often work together intricately.

Myth #11: You Have Only Five Senses

False. You have additional senses that give you more data about the world around you, including a sense of balance, pain, temperature, and passage of time.

Myth #12: You're Born with All the Brain Cells You'll Ever Have, Your Brain Is Hardwired, and Brain Damage Is Always Permanent

False. The brain remains plastic throughout life and can rewire itself in response to your experiences including trauma; it can also generate new brain cells under the right circumstances.

BRAINY FACTS

- Of the total blood and oxygen that is produced in our bodies, the brain steals 20 percent of it, despite being only roughly 2.5 percent of your body weight.

- Unlike with other organs, there can be no life without a brain, and as of yet, the brain cannot be transplanted. You have to work with the brain you were born with for the rest of your life. You might get a hip replaced, a heart stented, and a cancer removed, but you'll never get another brain.

- Your brain is roughly 73 percent water (same for your heart), and that is why it takes only 2 percent dehydration to affect your attention, memory, and other cognitive skills.

- Your brain weighs a little over three pounds. Sixty percent of the dry weight is fat, making the brain the fattiest organ in the body.

- All brain cells are not alike. There are many different types of neurons in the brain, each serving an important function.

- The brain is the last organ to mature. As any parent can attest, children's and teenagers' brains are not fully formed, which is why they take to risky behaviors and can have a harder time regulating their emotions. It isn't until about the age of twenty-five that the human brain reaches full maturity.

- Information to and from the brain travels faster than race cars, speeding up to more than 250 miles per hour.

- Your brain starts slowing down by the surprisingly young age of twenty-four, right before maximum maturity, but it peaks for different cognitive skills at different ages. No matter how old you are, you're likely still getting better at some things. An extreme case is vocabulary skills, which may peak as late as the early seventies!

PART TWO

A GUIDED TOUR OF THE KEEP SHARP PROGRAM WEEK BY WEEK

Welcome to the second part of the workbook. Here's where the action begins. Over the next 12 weeks, I'll lead you through activities and experiences aimed at sharpening your brain's functionality. They will be recommended in a specific sequence to build on each other. Because the brain is exceptionally plastic, it can rewire and reshape itself in a mere 12 weeks. It's like building any other muscle.

Okay, so the brain is not technically a muscle, but the analogy rings true: Like muscles in the body that atrophy and lose mass when underutilized, your brain needs to be "flexed" regularly to keep it strong, growing new neurons and building new networks. Just as we put healthy physical demands on our muscles to support muscle mass and tone, we need to put healthy demands on our brains that force them to think harder, problem solve better, and get creative (and wire new networks) when necessary. As noted in Myth #6, the "use it or lose it" dictum applies to both a real muscle and the metaphorical one that is your inner black box. The good news is the organ that is your brain responds remarkably well to practical strategies that promote its wellness.

You might be feeling overwhelmed or perhaps panicked at the thought of following this program if it means ditching some of your favorite foods, starting an exercise routine after having been sedentary for a long time, trying to find new ways to de-stress, and getting out of the house more often to socialize or convene with Mother Nature. I realize that for some people, nixing an addiction to sugar and breaking a sweat more often can be tough. Change is a challenge, and changing long-established habits takes concerted effort. You're wondering if this is truly doable in the real world. Well, let me repeat that you can do this. Take the plunge and experience the initial effects. Within the first two weeks, I predict that you'll have fewer anxious thoughts, better sleep, and improved energy. You'll feel clearer in the head, less moody, and hardier against daily stressors. Over time, you'll likely experience weight loss, and lab tests will show vast improvements in many areas of your biochemistry, including your metabolism and immune system.

It's smart to check with your doctor about beginning this program, especially if you have any health issues such as high blood pressure or diabetes. Never change any of your medications or other doctor-prescribed recommendations without consulting your physician. But do consider asking your doctor about getting some baseline testing done (see Week 9). As I've outlined, blood pressure, and levels of cholesterol, blood sugar, and inflammation all factor into risk for cognitive decline. You can often fight those numbers and bring them into a healthy range through this program and, when necessary, medications. Also, "knowing your numbers" (again, see Week 9) can serve as one of those motivators I mentioned earlier. When you know you have high blood pressure, for example, you know you have a goal to reach. The numbers or values concretize your journey more clearly.

This program will automatically help you to address these important areas, and I encourage you to re-check your numbers after you've gone through the program. I am certain you'll see improvements, but if not, that's when you may want to partner more rigorously with your doctor to figure out where you may have a special issue to address that's unique to your physiology. I know an individual whose oral microbiome, for example, was the chief culprit in underlying inflammation that in turn affected his cognition. No sooner did his treating physician send the patient to a periodontist to address his oral hygiene (and clean up his mouth's colonies of bacteria to support a healthy oral biome and calm down the inflammation) than his cognition improved and likely reduced his lifetime risk for serious brain decline and disease. Never underestimate the power of simple solutions.

Take this one day, one week, one change at a time. As a final reminder, you do not need to pursue this program precisely. All I ask is that you do what you can and aim to establish at least one new habit a week throughout these next 12 weeks. New habits can take time to get used to and become automatic in your daily life. That is why we're taking at least 12 weeks to cement these important practices and give you the time to experiment and tailor the strategies to your own lifestyle. Although some planning will be involved, such as scheduling workout times, searching for menu ideas and gathering ingredients, or getting friends together over a weekend, you can work these suggestions into your life as you see fit.

I won't be asking you to buy anything specific to make this program work for you. I'd love for you to invest in yourself, however. Maybe it is in the form of enrolling in a creative writing class, or joining a local yoga or dance studio, whatever aligns with your preferences. Customize this program to your needs and be honest about it. If I make a suggestion that you don't like, skip it or replace it with another. The goal of the recommendation will be clear, making it easier for you to adapt. I want this program to be flexible, doable, and personalized. Don't second-guess your ability to succeed at this; I've designed this program to be as practical and easy to follow as possible. And feel free to come back to Week 1 after you've completed all 12 weeks. This is a program you can do over and over again.

KICK-START IN YOUR KITCHEN

Over the past several years, I have focused on creating a style of eating that I can easily maintain even when I'm on the road, but it does require planning and commitment. You should strive to do the same, which might require learning new methods for grocery shopping and finding the best, freshest foods for you and your family that meets your budget. Spend time in your kitchen taking inventory and rethinking what's in your refrigerator and pantry.

Check off the following big box this week:

❏ **Reduce and Replace**

Reduce your intake of sugar-laden and artificially sweetened beverages, fast food meals, processed meats, highly salty foods, and sweets. Stop buying foods that a gardener or farmer (or your great-grandmother) wouldn't recognize.

Replace junk foods like potato chips and processed cheese dip with healthier alternatives such as raw nuts and veggie sticks with hummus. (By doing so, you lower trans fats and saturated fats while still having a satisfying snack. This is an easy hack and it turns out to be incredibly helpful to your brain.)

You can easily check off that big box simply by following my S.H.A.R.P. style of eating below—and avoid eating out this week.

S: SLASH THE SUGAR AND SALT, AND STICK TO YOUR ABCs

A-LIST FOODS TO CONSUME REGULARLY

Fresh vegetables (in particular, leafy greens such as spinach, chard, kale, arugula, collard greens, mustard greens, romaine lettuce, Swiss chard, turnip greens)

Whole berries

Fish and seafood

Healthy fats (e.g., extra virgin olive oil, avocados, whole eggs)

Nuts and seeds (unsalted)

B-LIST FOODS TO INCLUDE

Beans and other legumes

Whole fruits (in addition to berries)

Low-sugar, low-fat dairy (e.g., plain yogurt, cottage cheese)

Poultry

Whole grains

C-LIST FOODS TO AVOID OR LIMIT

Fried food

Pastries, sugary foods

Processed foods

Red meat (e.g., beef, lamb, pork, buffalo)

Red meat products (e.g., bacon)

Whole-fat dairy high in saturated fat, such as cheese and butter

Salt

SLAY PUBLIC ENEMY #1

Sugar is public enemy #1 to a healthy brain. How much sugar you consume relates directly to metabolic health, which then plays directly into brain health. Nearly 35 percent of all U.S. adults and 50 percent of those sixty years of age or older are estimated to have what's called metabolic syndrome, a combination of health conditions you don't want to have, such as obesity, high blood pressure, insulin resistance, type 2 diabetes, or a poor lipid profile (too much bad cholesterol, not enough good cholesterol).

Since 2005, researchers have found correlations between diabetes and Alzheimer's disease, especially when the diabetes is not controlled and a person suffers from chronic high blood sugar. As mentioned in Part One, some scientists have gone so far as to refer to Alzheimer's disease as "type 3 diabetes," because the disease often involves a disrupted relationship with insulin, the body's chief metabolic hormone. At the root of type 3 diabetes is the phenomenon that neurons in the brain become unable to respond to insulin, which means they can no longer absorb glucose, leading to cell starvation and death. Some researchers believe insulin deficiency or resistance is central to the cognitive decline of Alzheimer's disease and could be implicated in the formation of those infamous plaques that bungle up the brain's systems. People with type 2 diabetes—a disease characterized by the inability to manage healthy blood sugar levels—may be at least twice as likely to develop Alzheimer's disease, and those with prediabetes or metabolic syndrome may have an increased risk for having predementia or mild cognitive impairment (MCI), which often precedes dementia. But you don't need to have been diagnosed with type 2 diabetes to be on the path to Alzheimer's. In other words, studies are now showing that people with high blood sugar, regardless of a formal diagnosis of diabetes, have a higher rate of cognitive decline than those with normal blood sugar. The studies are clear: Get your blood sugar under control and avoid metabolic dysfunction—your brain (and your waistline) will thank you.[1] And the first thing you can do to support healthy metabolic function is to slash that sugar. In doing so, you'll likely slash a lot of salt as well.

10 WAYS TO SLASH SUGAR IN YOUR LIFE

1. Stop drinking beverages with sugar or artificial sugars, including soda, soft drinks, sweetened teas, energy and sports drinks, juices, shakes, and blended coffees.

2. Read and compare food labels and choose items with the lowest amount of added sugars. Added sugars should be clearly labeled. Watch out for sneaky code names for "sugar," as there are more than sixty names for it such as

brown rice syrup, corn syrup, fructose, fruit juice concentrate, dextrin, evaporated cane juice, ethyl maltol, barley malt, and caramel. Look for words that end in "-ose," syrups, "juices," and "concentrates." Also check out the Sugar-Science site maintained by the University of California, San Francisco: https://sugarscience.ucsf.edu/.

3. Use fresh fruit to top oatmeal, plain yogurt, pancakes, and so on, rather than liquid sugars and syrups.

4. Cook more at home and eat less frequently at restaurants. You get to control your ingredients. When you do eat out, patronize places where you have a good sense of their cooking styles and ingredients. Never hesitate to ask!

5. When baking, substitute unsweetened applesauce for sugar.

6. Don't keep processed sweets and baked goods in the house, such as muffins, pastries, bars, cookies, cakes, brownies, sweet rolls, doughnuts, pies, frozen dairy desserts, and candy. Most of those protein bars are packed with sugar.

7. Avoid fruit canned in syrup. Watch out for sugary sauces, condiments, dressings, spreads, jams, jellies, and preserves.

8. Experiment with new, natural sweeteners that have zero calories such as stevia, allulose, and monk fruit.

9. Prioritize sleep. Adequate high-quality sleep will help balance your hormones, keep your metabolism humming, and slash those sugar cravings.

10. Keep tabs on your stress. More stress means a stronger gravitational force toward sugar-laden foods and drinks.

H: HYDRATE SMARTLY

One of my mantras is "drink instead of eat." We often mistake hunger for thirst. Even moderate amounts of dehydration can sap your energy and disrupt your brain rhythm. Because our brains are not really that good at distinguishing thirst from hunger, if there is food around, we generally tend to eat. As a result, we walk around overstuffed and chronically dehydrated. Or we quench our thirst with the wrong drinks. Beverages are the leading category source of added sugars (47 percent of all added sugars). Let's see if we can avoid the brain-sapping beverages and drink brain-friendly ones this week.

Here's your cheat sheet:

- Drinks to ditch or severely limit (this should sound familiar): diet sodas, sweetened teas, energy drinks, blended coffees, milk shakes, smoothies, and juices (including pulverized vegetable drinks or pressed juices)

- Drinks to enjoy in moderation: coffee and tea, but cut yourself off from caffeinated beverages by 2:00 p.m. so as not to interrupt sleep

- Unlimited drinks: filtered fresh water—aim to drink half of your body weight in ounces daily (so if you weigh 150 pounds, that means drinking around 75 ounces)

- If you don't drink alcohol, don't start now. Recent studies have shown that alcohol reduces overall brain volume even at light-to-moderate consumption.[2] If you drink alcohol, drink in moderation. For men, doctors recommend they drink only up to two drinks a day (a drink is 12 ounces of beer, 5 ounces of wine, or 1.5 ounces—one shot glass—of liquor); for women it's one drink.

A: ADD MORE OMEGA-3 FATTY ACIDS FROM DIETARY SOURCES

The impact on the brain of omega-3 fatty acids from foods has been extensively studied, and a wealth of information links omega-3 fatty acids and a healthy brain. The best way to consume more natural omega-3s is to incorporate more of the following into your diet from food (the evidence is not established that supplements work the same!). Check some of these off your grocery store list this week:

- Raw, unsalted nuts: almonds, hazelnuts, walnuts, cashews

- Seeds: sesame, flax, hemp, pumpkin, chia, sunflower

- Whole olives

- Avocados

- Extra virgin olive oil. Canola, peanut, and avocado oils are high in omega-3s, but I prefer extra virgin olive oil in cooking and dressing dishes because it is rich in antioxidants, healthy monounsaturated fats, and compounds like polyphenols that are extra good for the brain. Many brands of extra virgin olive oil will make a "reserve" variety that's richer and has more robust, complex flavors from a more selective process of choosing which olives to use.

- Fatty fish: salmon, trout, herring, sardines, anchovies, albacore tuna, mackerel, oysters, Arctic char, black cod

When buying fish, know where it's coming from. Avoid fish from polluted waters or places where the mercury content in the fish can be too high. Mercury is a heavy metal that can harm the brain and is not easily eliminated from the body. The Monterey Bay Aquarium's Seafood Watch website (www.seafoodwatch.org) can help you choose the cleanest fish (wild or farmed) that are harvested with the least impact on the environment.

R: REDUCE PORTIONS

You can automatically rein in your portions by preparing meals yourself at home, using smaller plates, and avoiding second and third helpings. You know what you're putting into the meals you cook and have better control over ingredients and portion sizes. When possible, avoid frying and turn to boiling, poaching, steaming, or baking. This is yet another reason to cook more at home: You get to decide which method to use and control for those mystery oils, sauces, and added ingredients that come with food from restaurants. If you're at a restaurant, ask for a to-go container when you order. When your meal arrives, eyeball an adequate portion and put the rest in your box.

In *Keep Sharp*, I didn't thoroughly address fasting, but I want to share some new research that has emerged since its publication. It appears that the very act of restricting your calories, and I will define that in a moment, induces an altered metabolic state that, according to a 2019 review paper, "optimizes neuron bioenergetics, plasticity and resilience in a way that may counteract a broad array of neurological disorders."[3] The authors even boldly state: "Fasting improves cognition, stalls age-related cognitive decline, usually slows neurodegeneration, reduces brain damage and enhances functional recovery after stroke." The benefit may be coming entirely from just eating fewer calories, though another paper suggests limiting your calories creates surges of beneficial stem cells to replenish the cells unable to survive the fast. I don't think the data is strong enough to recommend one type of fasting over another, but there are generally four types of fasting ("intermittent fasting") to consider.

1. Time-restricted eating (the 16/8 or 14/10 split). In this option, you have set fasting and eating windows. For example, under the 16/8 protocol, you eat only within an eight-hour window and fast the remaining sixteen hours.

2. The twice-a-week method (the 5:2 method). Following this formula, you eat normally for five days per week, then on the other two days you reduce your calorie intake to a quarter of your daily needs. For most women, this means reducing your caloric load to about 500 calories per day; for men, it's about 600 calories. Do not fast on back-to-back days. Have regular eating days in between the fasting days. For example, Mondays and Thursdays can be the days you fast.

3. Alternate-day fasting. Using this method entails limiting calories every other day (again, restrict to 500 calories for women and 600 for men), and eating normally on the other days.

4. The twenty-four-hour fast (or eat: stop: eat method). Before trying a full twenty-four-hour fast, however, it's ideal to experiment with the previous options first and be sure to take into consideration any metabolic conditions you have. If you're diabetic, for example, you will want guidance on any kind of fasting regimen.

You should check with your doctor before trying any intermittent fasting protocol. Do not fast if you have a history of blood sugar problems, heart conditions, or eating disorders. There remains plenty of debate on intermittent fasting, with conflicting data and different outcomes in different people. Intermittent fasting can affect you in ways you may not expect so if you want to try it, ease into it and journal the experience in detail to document how you feel, how your hunger cues change, and whether or not you're getting what you want out of it (e.g., weight loss). It's not for everyone. Again, check with your doctor first.

Here's how to take the beginner's route: Simply start by cutting yourself off from food and caloric beverages by 7:00 p.m. (drinking water is okay) and skipping an early breakfast, delaying the morning meal to 11:00 a.m. By taking advantage of your natural overnight abstinence, it's practically effortless to reach a fasted state. Every hour after the twelve-hour fasting mark moves you toward better metabolic health. I try to only eat when the sun is shining, which is another guide to follow that helps you stick to a natural overnight fasting routine.

> *The best of all medicines are resting and fasting.*
>
> —Benjamin Franklin

P: PLAN AHEAD

Don't get caught starving without a meal or snack planned. This week, map out your meals below. I'll give you meal ideas beginning on page 80. You can pick and choose, or fill in your own blanks based on the above guidelines.

Day 1

Breakfast: _____

Lunch: _____

Snack: _____

Dinner: _____

Dessert: _____

Day 2

Breakfast: _____

Lunch: _____

Snack: _____

Dinner: _____

Dessert: _____

Day 3

Breakfast: _____

Lunch: _____

Snack: _____

Dinner: _____

Dessert: _____

Day 4

Breakfast: _____

Lunch: _____

Snack: _____

Dinner: _____

Dessert: _____

Day 5

Breakfast: _____

Lunch: _____

Snack: _____

Dinner: _____

Dessert: _____

Day 6

Breakfast: _____

Lunch: _____

Snack: _____

Dinner: _____

Dessert: _____

Day 7

Breakfast: _____

Lunch: _____

Snack: _____

Dinner: _____

Dessert: _____

BREAKFAST IDEAS

- Eggs (hard-boiled, soft-boiled, scrambled) with a side of colorful vegetables (roasted or sauteed with olive oil) and whole grain toast topped with a nut butter or slices of avocado

- Greek-style plain yogurt (with active live cultures) or steel-cut oatmeal topped with fresh berries, chopped walnuts or flaxseed, and a drizzle of honey

- Avocado toast with slices of smoked salmon or eggs

Tip: Avoid pastries, doughnuts, bagels, and cereals

LUNCH IDEAS

- Leafy green salad with lots of colors (e.g., broccoli, bell peppers, cucumber, pomegranate seeds, sliced strawberries, blueberries, chopped red onion, cherry tomatoes, celery) and a serving of healthy protein such as chicken, turkey, salmon, tuna, or tofu, topped with seeds, nuts, a drizzle of vinaigrette made with extra virgin olive oil and balsamic vinegar

- Roasted turkey, tuna fish, or chicken sandwich on whole grain bread or sourdough with a side of leafy greens (no chips) and a whole piece of fruit

- Vegan hummus wrap with vegetables and salad greens wrapped in a tortilla or flatbread with a side of fruit salad (e.g., small bowl of whole berries, cut melon, and apple slices)

Tip: Avoid burgers, fries, fast food, and buffet bars

SNACK IDEAS

- Whole fruit (e.g., banana, apple, pear, grapes, plum, peach)

- Handful of raw mixed nuts

- Chopped raw vegetables dipped in guacamole, hummus, tapenade, cottage cheese, or a nut butter

Tip: Avoid energy bars, chips, crackers, and candy

DINNER IDEAS

- Baked fish, turkey, or chicken with sides of roasted veggies and wild or brown rice

- Mixed vegetables (e.g., green beans, bell peppers, broccoli, asparagus, brussels sprouts, mushrooms) stir-fried in extra virgin olive oil with three to five ounces of grilled chicken, cold-water wild fish, or grass-fed steak with optional side of rice, quinoa, or couscous

- Vegan or turkey chili with a side salad

- Vegan or meat-based pasta dish with a side salad

Tip: Avoid takeout and ready-made meals

SIMPLE SIDE SALAD RECIPE

Baby organic arugula or other salad greens + roasted pine nuts + dollop of goat cheese + avocado slices + lots of juice from a lemon + shaved Parmesan + drizzle of extra virgin reserve olive oil.

DESSERT IDEAS

- A few squares of dark chocolate

- Fresh berries or fruit slices sprinkled with cinnamon

- Scoop (not a pint!) of ice cream or sorbet (you can find dairy-free varieties, too)

Tip: Avoid eating anything within two to three hours of bedtime

ADDED TIPS:

- Use vinegar, lemon, aromatic herbs, and spices to increase flavor in food without increasing salt content.

- Eat a rainbow of whole fruits and vegetables—a wide variety of different-colored produce. The nutrients and antioxidants that give green bell peppers or strawberries, for example, their colors are different from those that give red bell peppers or blueberries their hue.

- Explore your local farmers market and buy fresh foods.

- Frozen fruits and vegetables are perfectly fine to use in preparing meals, especially if they help you avoid processed ready-to-eat meals.

- Support your gut health (see top 10 list on the next page).

10 WAYS TO SUPPORT YOUR GUT HEALTH

1. Follow the S.H.A.R.P. protocol and start with slashing that sugar and salt (see page 70–71 for ten ideas).

2. Eat more fiber in the form of fresh whole fruits and vegetables (aim for 25 to 30 grams a day); star players include leeks, onions, asparagus, spinach, artichokes, broccoli, and other leafy greens.

3. Feed your gut bugs with sources of prebiotics: whole grains, apples, dandelion greens, bananas, asparagus, nuts, seeds, beans, lentils, chickpeas, leeks, and root vegetables such as Jerusalem artichokes (sunchokes), chicory root, garlic, and onions. Prebiotics are a type of undigestible fiber that serves as food for the bacteria, yeast, and other organisms in our body, helping to support good bacteria in the gut.

4. Consume more fermented foods (e.g., cultured yogurt, kimchi, pickles, kombucha tea, kefir). These foods always give me a boost, physically and cognitively (and it's not all in my head—studies show that fermented foods ultimately support a healthy microbiome that in turn has a positive effect on the brain).

5. Cut back on red meat, and when you do eat meat, buy the highest quality, leanest cuts possible (organic, grass-fed).

6. Get your movement in—movement keeps your digestion in motion and supports optimal microbiome composition.

7. Sleep soundly—a good night's sleep also promotes an ideal microbiome profile.

8. Use antibiotics only when necessary (not for the common cold). They have no benefit for viral infections and kill the good guys along with the bad guys. Taking too many antibiotics can destroy a healthy microbiome and allow the proliferation of certain strains of bacteria in the gut that you don't want in high numbers.

9. Stay hydrated with filtered, pure water.

10. Manage stress levels and make more time for you!

PERSONALIZE YOUR DIET

A few years ago I went to Kerala, India, to learn about the Ayurvedic diet. It's been around for thousands of years and is supposed to be personalized to balance the various energies in your body. With this way of eating, individuals are classified based on their "dosha" or body and personality type.

> *The body is the outcome of food. Even so, disease is the outcome of food. The distinction between ease and disease arises on account of wholesome nutrition or the lack of it, respectively.*
>
> —Charaka, one of the principal contributors to the ancient art and science of Ayurveda; born in the first century BCE, he is referred to as one of the founding fathers of medicine

DOSHAS, OR BODY TYPES

Pitta dosha—fire and water. Generally, these are people with medium physical build and short temper. They are advised to eat cooling, energizing foods and to minimize seeds, nuts, and spices.

Vata dosha—air and space. Energetic, with a light frame and more likely to have fatigue or anxiety when out of balance. The diet calls for warmer, grounding foods with few raw veggies, dried fruits, or bitter herbs. I was told I fit into this body type.

Kapha dosha—earth and water. People of this type are usually naturally calm, grounded with a sturdy frame but at higher risk of depression. Fruits, veggies, and legumes are a focus for them.

Whether or not you agree with this approach, I was particularly struck by the initial motivation behind the Ayurvedic diet. While most cultures focus on serving the palate first, the Ayurvedic diet determined the functional aspects of whole foods and then tailored them to people's specific body types. With that in mind, I do think there are certain foods that are ideal for your own productivity, as well as certain things to avoid. One way to really learn about what works for you is to be diligent about keeping a food journal. You'll find a template on the following page, but find a form that works for you, either on paper or on your mobile device.

FOOD JOURNAL

Date _____

BREAKFAST

LUNCH

DINNER

SNACKS

HYDRATION

NOTES (likes, dislikes, mood)

WHAT, NO SUPPLEMENTS?

Eating well means eating real food—not popping supplements.[4] While we all like the idea of a pill with the micronutrients neatly packaged in one swallow, that approach is not effective nor really possible. That bottle with broccoli on the label doesn't actually have broccoli in a pill. Some supplements can even be harmful. The evidence shows that micronutrients such as vitamins and minerals offer the greatest benefit when consumed as part of a balanced diet because all those other components in healthy food allow the micronutrients to be well absorbed and do their job better. It's called the entourage effect, and it is exactly what it sounds like.

You should also know that the supplement industry is woefully unregulated. As things stand now, supplement manufacturers do not have to test their products for effectiveness or safety. While there are some quality supplement makers with a solid and ethical track record, it's best to use supplements only under a doctor's recommendation. You cannot supplement your way out of a bad diet, and you should be able to get all the nutrition you need from real food.

When you record what you eat for a couple of weeks, really focus on how you feel thirty minutes later, a couple of hours later, and at night when you go to sleep. Pay close attention to the relationship between what you eat and how you experience that food throughout the day. For me, I learned fermented foods like pickles and kimchi were particularly good at increasing my productivity and creativity. Perhaps it is because I am nourishing my microbiome, and there is a significant connection between the gut and the brain. Be as diligent about your food journaling this week as possible and try to continue documenting your nutritional intake (including those cheats and sweets) for the entire 12 weeks. My hunch is that by the end of these 12 weeks, you'll have a newfound sense of what works for you and your body. This is why journaling your experience is important.

WEEK 1 NOTES

What I found helpful: _____

_____

What I found difficult: _____

_____

What I can improve upon: _____

_____

How I'm feeling in one to three words: _____

_____

Added Challenge: Go meatless on Mondays.

If you generally eat alone, invite a friend or neighbor over to cook with you and share a meal. This may push you outside your comfort zone, but that is the point. Give yourself extra credit if your guest is someone new, unexpected, or culturally different from you.

See if you can eat at least one meal with your nondominant hand. During the pandemic I started painting with my nondominant hand. Simply doing that for even a few minutes a day seems to activate my brain.

MOVE MORE

Movement is magic. It's free medicine available whenever you need it. And it's well established that cognitive improvements follow exercise. Movement increases the capacity of the heart, lungs, and blood to transport oxygen, which then helps boost the number of blood vessels and synapses, increasing brain volume, and decreasing age-related brain atrophy. Movement also nurtures new nerve cells and spurs increases in proteins that help those neurons survive and thrive. The result: positive effects in brain areas related to thinking and problem solving. The opposite is also true: inactivity is a disease unto itself. When you are sedentary, your muscles start to atrophy and certain signaling mechanisms in your body begin to slow down. Your body's own perimeter defenses, which help fight infections and mutated cells, no longer work as well, making your body vulnerable to infection and cancer. It's almost as if sitting sends a signal that this body is no longer worth inhabiting, and is close to the end of its life. Movement, especially things like brisk walking, sends a reminder that you are alive and want to stay that way.

WHERE AM I?

Last time I raised my heart rate and broke a sweat in physical movement for more than twenty minutes: _____

Physical activities I enjoy: _____

_____

Number of push-ups I can do without stopping to rest: _____

(Note: Minimum counts for good fitness is ten. It's okay if you need to start by doing them on your knees until you build that strength.)

On a scale of 1 to 10, how would I rank myself on the following:

- Cardio fitness (1 = low, 10 = high): _____
- Muscle strength (1 = low, 10 = high): _____

Overall fitness level: _____

1	5	10

←——————————————————————————————————→

(poor / couch potato)　(average/ room for improvement)　(seasoned athlete)

Unless you're already a "seasoned athlete" who prioritizes regular movement like taking regular showers, devote this week to two sessions of brisk neighborhood walks every day, once in the morning and once in the evening for twenty minutes each at a minimum. Multiple studies have definitively shown that walking at least thirty minutes per day is enough to reap significant physical, cognitive, and emotional benefits. This is in addition to any formal exercise you already do if you're not higher than 5 on the scale above. If you keep a regular routine and feel good about your level of fitness, see if you can try something different to surprise your body and use new muscles. If you're a jogger, for example, go swimming at a local rec center or sign up for a cycling or vinyasa flow yoga class. If you played tennis when you were younger, pick the game up again with friends or a local league, or try a related sport like paddle tennis or pickleball. Aim to increase your formal workouts to a minimum of thirty minutes a day, at least five days a week. You want to get your heart rate up by at least 50 percent of your resting baseline.

I also want you to engage in strength training two to three days this week but avoid back-to-back strength training days so you give your muscles time to recover. My eighty-year-old parents regularly do resistance training movements. When they began a regimen, I immediately noticed improvements in their posture, walking speed, and energy levels. You can buy some three-, five-, and eight-pound free weights (dumbbells) or resistance bands, or use your body weight as resistance and follow a program or class (live or prerecorded) streamed online from a screen. There's no excuse today since the pandemic inspired an explosion of online programming that doesn't require you to join a gym. On-demand and live-streamed fitness classes offered by companies such as Alo Moves, Apple Fitness+, Daily Burn, Glo, Obé Fitness, Peloton, and TheWKOUT gained popularity and you don't even need equipment for many classes. You can complete a successful sweat session with only your body, a water bottle, a towel, and ample space to move.

HOW FAST DO YOU WALK?

Surprise: Walking speed predicts longevity. It's a scientific fact now that people who keep up the pace as they age are likely to outlive those who slow down. And the increased risk of death starts at midlife: According to research led by Duke University, people who tend to walk more slowly at the age of forty-five demonstrate signs of premature accelerated aging, both physically and cognitively.[5] More specifically, those who walk at 1.8 miles per hour (33:20 minutes per mile) are likely to live the average life span for their age and gender whereas those who walk at 1.3 miles per hour (46:09 minutes per mile) are at greater risk for early mortality. The bottom line: Keep walking apace as you age! Your gait speed is something you can easily measure and is a pretty good indicator of health or, conversely, decline. Intensify your walks by using walking sticks or poles to engage more of your upper body and core. Using poles on flat terrain or downhill can in fact help take some of the pressure off the lower extremities and prevent joint issues in the knees and ankles.

For those who haven't busted a move in a while, it's time to get going. Start gently and work your way up to more rigorous routines. If you've been totally sedentary, start with five to ten minutes of burst exercise (thirty seconds of maximal effort and ninety seconds of recovery) and work up to twenty minutes at least three times per week. This is also called HIIT (high-intensity interval training) and has been shown to provide multiple health benefits that of course include boosting brain power (and elevating levels of BDNF to spur new brain cells).[6] Remember, prolonged intense activity will release cortisol, which can be detrimental to BDNF, but short bursts with recovery can be very effective. You can do this any number of ways: walking outside and varying your speed and levels of intensity with hills; using classic gym equipment such as treadmills and StairMasters; jumping rope; or taking online exercise classes to perform a routine in the comfort of your home (most of these require a fee or monthly subscription, but they offer free trial sessions so you can find the one you like the best). You can find plenty of free videos to follow on YouTube alone.

Remove barriers to regular movement by planning how and when you will work out. Get out your calendar and schedule your physical activities. (If you prefer first thing in the morning, make your a.m. walk the cooldown at the end; if evenings are your time for more rigorous movement, use the p.m. walk to wind down afterward.) Mix up your routines. On Monday, Wednesday, and Friday, for example, you might go for a cardio-based class online and stream a yoga class on Tuesday and Thursday. Then, use Saturday to go for a hike with friends and then make Sunday your rest day. The goal is to have addressed all four of the following categories each week through your chosen activities: 1) cardio; 2) strength; 3) flexibility; and 4) coordination and balance. Use the following page as your template.

DAILY MOVEMENT LOG			
Date and Time	**Activities** (cardio, strength, flexibility, coordination and balance)	**Total Time**	**Notes** (feelings, likes, dislikes, ideas for future activities)

As I mentioned, I try to break a sweat every day, aiming for about an hour of brisk movement in addition to as much natural movement as possible throughout the day. My go-tos are either swimming, cycling, or running, and I throw in dedicated strength training a few times a week as well. As a father of three girls with a demanding job, I still find a way to fit this type of routine in every day. Human behavior dictates that you will fill whatever time you are given to complete a task, and people think of "exercise" as the first expendable thing when they get busy and want another hour of time for something else. I just don't do that; exercise is sacred time on my schedule. Wherever I am in the world, I have my running shoes, swimsuit, goggles, and resistance bands. And, at the recommendation of my chair of neurosurgery, Dr. Dan Barrow, I do a hundred push-ups every day.

For me, convenience is critically important. I make all this accessible by having certain tools within easy reach. For example, I keep weights in my bedroom, and I've got a doorframe pull-up bar at home and in my office. Incidentally, pull-ups are a great way to build your back muscles and strengthen your core. They are hard at first, but you start to feel the payoff almost immediately. People often neglect upper body strength, especially as they get older, but it's good for posture, bone density, and metabolism, and it even helps your lungs ward off pneumonia, especially if you find yourself in a hospital or bedridden. Ideally, each week you'll have gotten enough movement in to address all four areas:

- ❑ Cardio
- ❑ Strength
- ❑ Flexibility
- ❑ Coordination and balance

MAKE MOVEMENT SOCIAL

Don't underestimate the power of a group setting for movement and exercise. Make them a social experience. A recent Danish study found that adults who played team sports lived longer than people who were sedentary.[7] Games like tennis and other racquet sports consistently add more years to life than solo endeavors like cycling or running.[8] Sports that require multiple players offer a double bonus, so think about:

- Enlisting a friend in your exercise routine for one day this week.

- Joining a walking or running group or asking a coworker to go with you for a fast stroll at lunchtime.

- Checking out Active.com for a list of local groups and activities for you and your family. The site also offers a directory of virtual programs in your geographical area. Meetup.com also can be a source for finding nearby group walks and hikes.

NO TIME TO BUST A MOVE?

As I said from the start, I believe in movement, not exercise. If you have a day with absolutely no time for formal exercise, then think about the ways you can get in more minutes of physical activity during that day. The goal is to walk, stand, and move our bodies enough to counteract the harm that can result from sitting for most of the day. Some ideas:

- When you are short on time, break up your routine and think of ways to combine your movement with other tasks; for example, conduct a meeting with a colleague at work while walking outside, or stream your favorite show while you complete a set of yoga poses on the floor. This is a beneficial form of multitasking—the brain can handle physical movement while thinking about other things. New research indicates that you can also achieve these same health benefits from doing three ten-minute bouts of exercise as you would from doing a single thirty-minute workout.

- Limit the minutes you spend sitting down. Every time you are about to sit, ask yourself: "Can I stay standing and moving instead?" Walk around while you talk on the phone, take the stairs rather than the elevator, and park a distance away from the front door to your building.

- Simply make a point to get up every hour for a five-minute stroll or jog in place and then do some burpees (search the web if you don't know what a burpee is). The more you move throughout the day, the more your body and brain benefit.

HOW MUCH IS ENOUGH?

According to the Centers for Disease Control and Prevention, fully 80 percent of Americans don't get enough regular exercise.[9] Only about a quarter (23 percent) of adults meet the recommended requirements. Those requirements are defined as at least 150 minutes of moderate-intensity aerobic physical activity or 75 minutes of vigorous-intensity physical activity, or an equivalent combination each week. For people aged sixty-five and older, the numbers are bleak: less than 40 percent of people engage in at least 150 minutes of physical activity per week, and 20 percent don't do any type of formal exercise.

WEEK 2 NOTES

What I found helpful: _____

_____

What I found difficult: _____

_____

What I can improve upon: _____

_____

How I'm feeling in one to three words: _____

_____

Added Challenge: Create your own playlist to motivate your exercise prep and execution. When I put my playlists together for exercise, I have a few specific goals. I want a beat that helps regulate my movements. The music should be uplifting, and even distracting to take my mind off how much I'm pushing my body. Finally, this music should be something that helps my brain process fatigue and keeps me motivated.

For this music, I pick songs with 120–140 beats per minute and strong affirming lyrics. While I will often put more familiar songs on my workout playlist, I make it a point of not listening to that playlist outside of my workouts, so as to not get desensitized to it.

Below is a sample playlist of old and newer tunes that get me going:

SANJAY'S MUSIC TO GET MOVING

"Eye of the Tiger" (theme from *Rocky*), Survivor

"Extreme Ways," Moby

"Cold Heart," Elton John and Dua Lipa

"Blinding Lights," The Weeknd

"Shape of You," Ed Sheeran

"Stronger," Kelly Clarkson

"Human," The Killers

"I Will Wait," Mumford & Sons

"Just Like Fire," Pink

"Don't Start Now," Dua Lipa

"Midnight" (Giorgio Moroder Remix), Coldplay

"Diablo Rojo," Rodrigo y Gabriela

"I Gotta Feeling," Black Eyed Peas

"Put a Little Love in Your Heart," Al Green and Annie Lennox

"Modern Love," David Bowie

"On Top of the World," Imagine Dragons

"Wake Me Up" Avicii

"Raging" (featuring Kodaline), Kygo

"Jump," The Pointer Sisters

"Feel It Still," Portugal. The Man

"Style," Taylor Swift

"Fireball" (featuring John Ryan), Pitbull

"Best Friend," Sofi Tukker

"Woke Up in Bangkok," Deepend & YouNotUs

"About Damn Time," Lizzo

"Let's Get Loud," Jennifer Lopez

"Locked Out of Heaven," Bruno Mars

"Viva La Vida," Coldplay

"Love on the Weekend," John Mayer

"Home," Phillip Phillips

"Sanctuary," Cure

"Outtasite," Wilco

"Young Forever," Jay-Z

"Just Breathe," Pearl Jam

"Shotgun," George Ezra

"California Sun," Ramones

"Crazy in Love," Beyoncé

CULTIVATE BEAUTY SLEEP FOR YOUR BRAIN

How well did you sleep last week? Last night? Do you remember dreaming? Did you sleep solidly without waking? Do you rely on an alarm to wake you up? Again, most adults need seven to nine hours a night. How close are you to that?

Sleep is medicine. I sorely underestimated the value of sleep for far too long and wish I could gain back all those hours—which probably amounts to years—that I lost. Now I make sleep one of my highest priorities and it's time you did too by following these 5 rules for a good night:

#1 GOOD NIGHT RULE: STICK TO A SCHEDULE

Go to bed at the same time every day. Avoid "social jet lag," which happens when you sleep in after a late night. Irregular sleep patterns are detrimental to health. In the morning, expose your eyes to sunlight, as this will help set your body clock. Everything about our evolutionary biology and neuroscience makes the critical importance of mornings clear. Simply put: We are hardwired to get up early and absorb the rising sun. Don't stay up past midnight. Notice when you first feel sleepy and adjust your schedule accordingly. The best bedtime is when you feel most sleepy before midnight. NREM (non-rapid eye movement) sleep tends to dominate sleep cycles in the early part of the night. As night moves closer to dawn, dream-rich REM sleep begins to take over. Although both types of sleep are important and offer separate benefits, NREM, slow wave sleep is deeper and more restorative than REM sleep. Note that your ideal bedtime will likely change as you age. The older you get, the earlier your bedtime will be and the earlier you will naturally wake up, but the overall number of hours you sleep should not change.

#2 GOOD NIGHT RULE: AVOID LONG NAPS LATE IN THE DAY

The evidence on whether naps are beneficial to brain health in adults is still unclear. Some people swear by short power naps (twenty minutes or so), but it also can be a signal that you're not sleeping well at night, and as a result upping your risk for problems that tie directly into brain health. A large study that came out in 2022, for instance, found that people who often nap have a greater chance of developing high blood pressure and having a stroke.[10] If you're a napper, limit napping to thirty minutes in the early afternoon, say before 3:00 p.m. Longer naps later in the day can disrupt nighttime sleep. If you're someone who is trying to increase your nighttime sleep to at least seven hours, skip the nap entirely. You won't be able to suddenly sleep for seven to nine hours overnight, as it will take time for your body to adjust and get used to a new schedule, so be patient. If you feel sleepy during the day but want to avoid napping, take a walk in fresh air and get your body moving. Notice if something you ate dragged you down or perhaps your body needs some nourishment. Make sure you are hydrated adequately, and aren't feeling any early signs of thirst. Try a light snack—a piece of whole fruit or a handful of nuts—and then step outside for a brisk walk.

HOW TO LENGTHEN YOUR SLEEP TIME NATURALLY

If you're not sleeping long enough, don't expect to fix that overnight (pun intended). Make adjustments in fifteen- or thirty-minute increments over the next several weeks. Choose which side of the cycle—bedtime or wake time—to shift. For most people, it's easier to be more flexible with bedtime than wake time. Dial back your bedtime routine by fifteen minutes for a few days, then dial it back another fifteen minutes for a total of thirty minutes from your original bedtime. Maintain that routine for another several days until you feel ready to trim back another fifteen minutes. Repeat that until you reach a fully blocked sleep time of seven to nine hours.

#3 GOOD NIGHT RULE: WATCH WHAT YOU EAT AND DRINK LATE IN THE DAY

Avoid caffeine after lunch (definitely after 2:00 p.m.), and don't eat or drink for two to three hours before bed to keep from waking up to use the bathroom. Heavy meals too close to bedtime can also disrupt sleep.

#4 GOOD NIGHT RULE:
MIND YOUR MEDICINES

Pharmaceuticals, whether over-the-counter or prescribed, can contain ingredients that affect sleep. For example, many headache remedies contain caffeine. Some medicines for the common cold can have stimulating decongestants (such as pseudoephedrine). Side effects of many widely used drugs such as antidepressants, steroids, beta blockers, and medicines for Parkinson's can all affect sleep too. Be aware of what you are taking, and if they are medicines you must take, check with your doctor to see if you can take them earlier in the day when they will have the least impact on sleep.

#5 GOOD NIGHT RULE:
SET THE SETTING

Keep your room cool, quiet, dark, and electronic-free (do not take your phone to bed with you unless you have it in a mode that's not emitting light or sending you notifications!). The ideal temperature for sleeping is between 60 and 67 degrees Fahrenheit. Consider a sleep mask if it is not possible to black out your environment. Try a sound machine or white noise generator to block out noises from the street if you live in an urban environment. And keep pets out of the bedroom if they disrupt your sleep by moving around or making noise. Establish bedtime rituals by setting aside at least thirty minutes to an hour for unwinding and performing tasks that help your body know that bedtime is coming soon. This means disconnecting from stimulating tasks (such as working, being on the computer, or using your cell phone) and engaging in activities that are calming such as taking a warm bath, reading, drinking herbal tea, or listening to soothing music. Stretch or do something relaxing. Wearing socks to keep your feet warm can also help you fall asleep more easily.

Again, avoid any bright screens, especially those that emit blue light, which is a wavelength of light that can powerfully suppress melatonin—the hormone necessary for sleep. Blue light is disruptive to sleep and your body's sleep-wake cycle. You can buy screen filters or wear special glasses that block blue wavelengths, but these are not as effective as previously thought.[11] There's no evidence that shows blue-blocking lenses or filters make any difference. Ideally, you should avoid screens within an hour of bedtime and find other ways of winding down that don't entail a screen or digital device.

SLEEP LOG

	Current	Goal
Time to bed	_____	_____
Time awake	_____	_____
Hours of sleep	_____	_____

Rules I need to work on to get to my goal _____

_____

_____

WEEK 3 NOTES

What I found helpful: _____

_____

What I found difficult: _____

_____

What I can improve upon: _____

_____

How I'm feeling in one to three words: _____

_____

LET TECH HELP YOU GET "HIGH-TECH SLEEP"

Some people love to use technology to aid in their sleep. The number of devices and products hitting the multibillion-dollar sleep-aid market is phenomenal. From high-tech smartwatches and rings that can track the quality and quantity of your sleep to apps that offer a wide selection of stories and meditations for bedtime, there's no shortage of sleep-enhancing supplies. Wearable devices can track your sleep at night and can tell you how well you've slept and even when you hit deep sleep and for how long throughout the cycles. You can also learn the time it takes for you to fall asleep and get a 360-degree picture of your sleep quality. This allows you to then use the data to tweak certain things the next day—your nutrition and caffeine intake, for example, and when you exercise—to see if that changes your sleep experience. These technologies are not for everyone, but I encourage you to explore what might work for you and take the challenge!

Added Challenge: Schedule a sleep study if you think you have a sleep disorder that requires treatment. Do this if you have at least three of the following symptoms:

- trouble falling or staying asleep three times a week for at least three months

- frequent snoring

- persistent daytime sleepiness

- leg discomfort before sleep

- acting out your dreams during sleep

- grinding your teeth

- waking with a headache or aching jaws

Call your doctor for a referral. Many sleep centers have a way of allowing you to do the study in your own home and then sending your data to the center for analysis. If you have concerns about conditions like sleep apnea, your insurance may cover it. Many hospitals offer these services.

FIND YOUR TRIBE

Imagine what life would be like without anyone else around you. I know I've made it clear you need to put yourself first on this program, but that also means connecting with others and strengthening the bonds you have with important people in your life today as well as individuals who will likely come into your life in the future. If you don't already have a robust and diverse circle of friends, make room to expand it. Far too many people lose connections through the years and lack strong social relationships by the time they hit midlife and beyond. This is especially true once children have grown up and live on their own, and people who used to be part of your life have passed on.

We tend to underestimate the value in casually reaching out to people in our social circles.[12] The mere act of saying a brief "hello" and asking someone how they are doing through a phone call, email, or text can be surprisingly meaningful. In 2022, a team of researchers at the University of Pittsburgh put this to the test by running a series of experiments that showed we indeed underestimate how much friends appreciate hearing from us.[13] And the most powerful, meaningful check-ins were the ones people hadn't expected because they hadn't been in contact with each other recently. In all the experiments, which involved nearly 6,000 participants, the person who initiated contact significantly underestimated how much their gesture would be appreciated. The study included contact between individuals who considered their friendship to be weak. Small moments of connection matter, even if it's time-consuming or awkward. Other research shows that positive social interactions are linked with a sense of purposefulness in older adults.[14] These findings further highlight the need to connect with others on a daily basis to function well and feel our best. Friendship and fellowship are key pieces to personal health just like eating and sleeping. And at a time when loneliness looms large in society, each one of us must do our part to stay connected—and help others do the same.

I once met a man in his eighties who had long since retired and become so isolated by his age and lack of mobility that he could not name a single person to dine with on his birthday. He had no spouse, no children, and no close relatives, and he lived alone in the big old house in which he had grown up. When I met him, he wanted to downsize to a smaller place but didn't know where to begin and had no one to call for help. I sensed a sadness and a deep regret for having let life go by like that. You'd be surprised by how many individuals can end up in such a situation. Lacking social connection can be as destructive as any biological problem to cognition and overall well-being.[15] In fact, in a large review study that crunched the numbers and controlled for confounding factors, social isolation corresponded to a nearly 30 percent increased likelihood of death.[16] Let's aim to work on those connections, and we'll start with a few exercises here this week.

EXERCISE 1

List a few important people in your life today you can rely on when things get tough. I have a younger brother, Suneel, who has always been one of my closest confidants in addition to my wife. Identify these types of people in your life, and celebrate them. Cultivate those relationships with intention, and realize they need to be nurtured just like anything else you value in life. In his book *Backable*, Suneel (yes, he's also a writer!) writes about the four types of people you should think about in your tribe, the four Cs. These are just guidelines but may help you start thinking about your relationships (and you can certainly have more than one person who fills a category).

The **Collaborator** is someone who's going to help you expand your thoughts and practice how to deliver your ideas. They're not going to agree with everything you say, but their feedback is going to be constructive. When you're with a Collaborator, you feel like you're in a musical jam session—riffing off each other and lifting your ideas.

Who is your Collaborator? _____

The **Cheerleader** is the person who is going to make you feel confident before you get in the room. Hockey players will warm up their goalie before a game with practice shots that are easy to block. The objective, in those final minutes, is to build the goalie's confidence, not his skill.

Who is your Cheerleader? _____

The **Coach** will help you figure out if your thinking or idea is right for *you*. Remember, just because an idea is a good fit for the outside world doesn't mean it's a good fit for you. My wife, Rebecca, is my coach.

Who is your Coach?

_____

The **Cheddar** is the most important role in your circle. (The name comes from a character in the film *8 Mile* that is one of Eminem's friends who likes to play devil's advocate.) Your Cheddar is the person who will deliberately poke holes in your ideas, be brutally honest, and offer suggestions that at times may feel unsettling.

Who is your Cheddar? _____

These are the core members of your tribe—the people who are there for you no matter what, when you're celebrating your greatest victories or at your most vulnerable. These are the comrades you keep who won't judge you no matter how messy life gets. Think about what they bring to your life and write down those details.

_____

_____

_____

As you do this exercise, you might think of individuals who drain you or bring you down emotionally. You can name them here and distance yourself from them.

_____

_____

_____

We can't always evict certain people from our lives, but we can certainly limit their impact.

EXERCISE 2

Write a letter to the person who holds your #1 spot for being your trusty companion in life. It does not have to be a spouse. Write about their importance to your well-being and express your gratitude for their contributions to your health and happiness. Bonus: Extend an invitation to get together soon over a meal or outdoor excursion.

EXERCISE 3

Look through your photographs of you with loved ones through the years and pick at least three that reflect moments of pure joy and connection. Print them out and paste here:

WEEK 4 NOTES

What I found helpful: _____

_____

What I found difficult: _____

_____

What I can improve upon: _____

_____

How I'm feeling in one to three words: _____

_____

Added Challenge: Think of someone from your past with whom you've lost touch. Reach out to them via email, phone, or text. Find time to catch up!

BE A STUDENT OF LIFE

How often are you reading books and learning about topics outside your professional interest? If you're a nonfiction fan, when was the last time you devoured a cannot-put-down or whodunit novel? Have you wanted to learn a new language? Take a painting, computer coding, or cooking class? Join a writing group to finish that memoir of yours? Go skydiving, scuba diving, deep sea or fly fishing, or climb a mountain? Return to a sport that you used to play in your youth? Try a totally new activity that pushes your boundaries?

When you're a "student" of life, who ushers in new information and stimuli, your brain is forced to respond and work in ways that build new networks, strengthen old ones, and make fresh memories. It also compels you to pay more attention, which is key to brain health. Memory difficulties can, in fact, be simply the result of poor attention skills. And there's no better way to work on those skills than to immerse yourself in something different or that rekindles a long-lost habit. Even a neglected hobby can be revisited and experienced like you've never done it before. And novels, by the way, can be excellent brain games in and of themselves because they compel you to manage characters and complicated plots in your head. When people develop cognitive decline, they often abandon intricate fictional tales because they can be too hard to read—to effortlessly follow and keep up with the story line. Nobody thinks they are pushing cognitive boundaries when they read a good book, but the essence of reading and "digesting" a narrative is doing just that.

Now's the time to make this happen. Regardless of the activity, it is all part of keeping sharp. I don't expect you to sign up for a new class right away or jump out of a plane tomorrow, but begin to explore the possibilities. Check out the local college's adult education courses, or maybe your local rec center has programs. Preferably, do something that nudges you outside your comfort zone. And, if you can add a motor component to the activity such as playing music, painting, pottery, even better. Start by asking yourself the following questions:

Things I'd like to try:

_____

_____

Hobbies or sports from my youth I'd like to rekindle:

_____

_____

Books I'd like to read (list from both nonfiction and fiction categories):

_____

_____

When I plan anything from a trip to a dinner party, I find myself researching specific people and places. I think of it as learning with a purpose. Before a recent trip to Japan, I not only read about the customs of the country and the genesis of those customs, but I also read several novels from Japanese writers like Yasunari Kawabata, Ruth Ozeki, and Haruki Murakami. Allowing myself to learn as much as I can about a specific topic for an upcoming event has served as a good source of new wisdom. So, with that in mind, think about cultures or people you'd like to learn more about and write down how you can get up close and personal with them:

_____

_____

_____

_____

WEEK 5 NOTES

What I found helpful: _____

_____

What I found difficult: _____

_____

What I can improve upon: _____

_____

How I'm feeling in one to three words: _____

_____

Added Challenge: Buy a book today that helps you learn more about something unfamiliar to you. And craft a vision board with the ideas you listed this week using cutouts from magazines or other publications that act as visual cues. A vision or "dream" board is a collage of pictures and words that represents your wishes, dreams, and goals. You can create one simply by using a posterboard or dedicating a wall in your home to feature your gallery. Vision boards are meant to motivate and inspire you to take the steps toward realizing your objectives in life—especially the hard-to-reach or challenging ones.

ACTIVATE ANTIDOTES TO STRESS

A few years ago, I worked on a documentary for HBO called *One Nation Under Stress*. It was a film focused on understanding the root causes of stress for so many Americans. Something that really stuck with me was the idea that stress itself is not the enemy. In fact, we all need stress to get out of bed, study for a test, and get through our day. The problem is chronic stress—the type that never ends and that wears us down both emotionally and physically.

I took away two important lessons from my documentary. First, I use the times of stress to turbocharge through challenges. Instead of getting paralyzed or weakened by stress, I now realize how it can galvanize my thoughts and increase my energy. Second, I break the cycle of relentless stress. That means authentic real breaks from stressors. While I like music and exercise, and I prefer to engage in activities around water as much as possible, the biggest benefit comes when I truly turn off the devices and let my mind wander free without an agenda. Some of my happiest, least stressful times were simply open blank spaces on the calendar that allowed me to have a sense of control because I was not feeling rushed or at the whims of an overly busy schedule. When you're calm and collected, you naturally feel more in control of life and what's in front of you. Which brings me to ask the question: How much control do you feel you have over your life today? Find a number between 1 and 10:

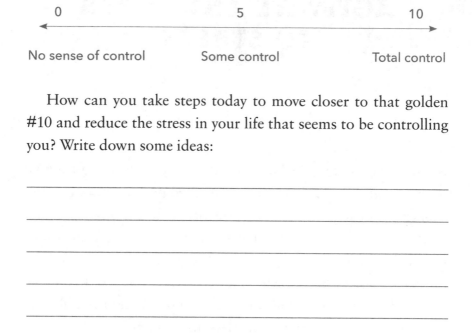

How can you take steps today to move closer to that golden #10 and reduce the stress in your life that seems to be controlling you? Write down some ideas:

_____

_____

_____

_____

_____

Now I'll give you some of my own:

MEDITATION

After spending time with the Dalai Lama a few years ago at the Drepung Monastery in Mundgod, India, I began a daily meditation habit. Rather than practicing a traditional form of meditation that has me focus on a single object, words, music, or my breath, I learned a type of analytical meditation in which I think about a problem I'm trying to solve and place it in an imaginary clear bubble. Then, with my eyes closed, I see the problem floating weightlessly in front of me, and as it rises, I watch it disentangle from other attachments, including my emotions. I can more easily bring logic into the picture and solve the problem reasonably without distractions. I've meditated this way every day since 2017. The first two minutes, as I create my thought bubble and let it float above me, are still the hardest. After that, I reach what can best be described as that quintessential flow state, in which twenty to thirty minutes pass easily. I am more convinced than ever that even the most ardent skeptics can find success with analytical meditation.

If you don't already meditate, find the type of meditation that works for you. Plenty of apps are available today to help you get into a relaxed state or take you through a guided meditation exercise. Try a few this week and see what resonates with you. At the very least, I encourage you to practice deep breathing twice daily. A deep breathing exercise that takes minutes is probably the simplest and most doable type of meditation you can do anywhere. It will get you started and give you a foundation for trying more advanced techniques. In addition to my analytical meditation, I do deep breathing exercises daily as a behavioral hack to turn the volume down on my stress. All you have to do is sit comfortably in a chair or on the floor, close your eyes, and make sure your body is relaxed—releasing all tension in your neck, arms, legs, and back. Inhale through your nose for as long as you can, feeling your diaphragm and abdomen rise as your stomach moves outward. Take in a little more air when you think you've reached the top of your lungs. Slowly exhale to a count of twenty, pushing every breath of air from your lungs. Continue for at least five rounds of deep breaths.

10 MENTAL HEALTH APPS
TO CALM YOUR MIND

BetterHelp	Moodfit
Calm	MoodMission
Happify	Sanvello
Headspace	Shine
iBreathe	Talkspace

If you think about your sympathetic and parasympathetic nervous systems, deep breathing exercises will make even more sense. When our sympathetic system is activated, we often feel stressed. It is our fight-or-flight system activating. A quick way to counter that feeling is by activating your parasympathetic system by taking a few deliberate deep breaths. It almost seems too easy, but within a short time you can bring your body and brain into better balance. If you can think about things for which you are grateful at the same time, even better (more on this shortly). It is almost impossible to carry both toxicity and gratitude in your brain at the same time.

Meditation in any form is not for everyone, but let's see if you can find at least one stress-reducing strategy to practice once a day for at least fifteen minutes. If not meditation, perhaps it's prayer, tai chi, guided imagery, progressive muscle relaxation, restorative yoga, or journal writing. To get some ideas going in your mind, answer the following questions:

I find most joy and sense of calm when: _____

_____ .

I lose a sense of time when: _____

_____ .

I am most relaxed when: _____

_____ .

I feel the most mindful, present, and at peace when: _____

_____ .

My happy places: _____

_____ .

NATURE THERAPY

One of my favorite things to do is go on a fast-paced walk outside in nature where I make an effort to take in the surroundings and pay attention to as many visual details as I can find. I also take in the smells and sounds. For me, this isn't a workout, it is a *play-out*. I get exposed to nature's noises and even some substances like phytoncides (more on this shortly), which helps me overcome obstacles like writer's block. I don't listen to music or a podcast; I'm totally immersed in Mother Nature. She has curative powers.

The Japanese take nature therapy seriously and even have a name for it: forest bathing, or *shinrin-yoku*—which means just being in the presence of trees. Forest bathing has been popular lately throughout the world as a way to lower heart rate and blood pressure and reduce stress hormone production. While spending time in nature has long been recommended to improve mental well-being, we now know exactly why. When you are forest bathing, breathing in the "aroma of the forest," you are also absorbing good chemicals known as phytoncides, which protect trees from insects and other stressors. As we have learned over the past decade, these phytoncides can also protect us by increasing our natural killer immune cells and decreasing cortisol levels.

You needn't travel to a far-off wooded forest; you can do well just by digging in the dirt of your own garden or visiting a local park or beach. Some research has found that walking in nature, as opposed to walking in urban environments, may help people manage stress, calm rumination, and regulate emotion. A number of studies have found that green spaces and parks in cities are linked to positive mental health. I spend a lot of time indoors—in windowless operating rooms and newsrooms—so I cherish the times I can roam and play outside and absorb the pleasures of nature.

WORRY JOURNALING

Next to my bed, I have a notepad and one of my favorite pens. If there is anything bothering me, I simply write it down and place a little box next to it to cross off when it's over or I've completed a task. Simply writing down the task eases the cognitive demand of trying to remember it. Sometimes, I can come up with solutions to address the problem and write that down too. Try it!

GRATITUDE JOURNALING

On the flip side of the worry coin is gratitude. See if you can begin and end your day by thinking of things for which you are grateful and consider keeping a gratitude journal. Research finds that gratitude reduces depression and anxiety, lowers stress, and increases happiness and empathy. It is hard to be angry or distressed when you are practicing gratitude. My active gratitude practice is a big part of giving my brain a timeout. It acts like a big reset button on my brain and lets the less significant issues (that drain my brain) melt away. I do this myself and with my family every day I can. See if you can begin or end your day this week by thinking of at least three things for which you are grateful, and consider keeping a gratitude journal using the same prompt below over the course of the next seven days.

List three things you're grateful for today (Day 1):

1. _____

2. _____

3. _____

List three things you're grateful for today (Day 2):

1. _____

2. _____

3. _____

List three things you're grateful for today (Day 3):

1. _____

2. _____

3. _____

List three things you're grateful for today (Day 4):

1. _____

2. _____

3. _____

List three things you're grateful for today (Day 5):

1. _____

2. _____

3. _____

List three things you're grateful for today (Day 6):

1. _____

2. _____

3. _____

List three things you're grateful for today (Day 7):

1. _____

2. _____

3. _____

TACKLE YOUR DAY LIKE A SURGEON

Are you a proud multitasker? Well, it might be killing your brain. Contrary to our attempts to manage multiple tasks at the same time, the brain doesn't like to do that (unless, as noted earlier, one of those tasks is movement). Sure, you can walk and talk at the same time while breathing and digesting your lunch, but the brain can't concentrate on executing two activities that demand conscious effort, thinking, comprehension, or skill. When you try to mentally multitask, you slow down your thinking. While it might seem like you're being more productive, everything takes longer to accomplish. Would you want me operating on your brain while I dictate an email or take a phone call? The brain handles tasks sequentially but can switch attention between them so quickly that we're given the illusion that we can perform multiple tasks simultaneously.

If you want to get more done using less effort, aim to work on what's called your attentional ability: focus and concentrate on one sequence—one task—at a time and avoid distractions. This can be a surprisingly joyous experience—one that I have whenever I am in the operating room. The OR is one of the few places where distractions aren't allowed. You are scrubbed, unable to check your phone as you enter a fully focused state on the task in front of you. It is like taking your turbo-powered brain on an empty flat road and letting it rip. Most of the time, our brains are stuck in stop-and-go traffic, working hard and moving sluggishly amid competing demands and drains on our attention. Let your brain focus on one thing at a time. You will not only get more done than you thought possible, but you will also achieve a level of bliss that is tough to replicate. The brain loves the rhythm of working in sequences—not everything all at once. It also helps with sanity!

To that end, see if you can take one thing off your To Do list each day this week:

Day 1: _____

Day 2: _____

Day 3: _____

Day 4: _____

Day 5: _____

Day 6: _____

Day 7: _____

If you struggle to come up with at least one thing, here's a way to think about planning your daily tasks: Identify your marbles and sand. If you have a jar that you are filling with marbles and sand, which do you put in first? The marbles. Then you can allow the sand to fill the spaces in between. This is a key metaphor for planning your day and maximizing your time. Think of the marbles as the important blocks of your day (appointments, commitments, projects, important tasks including movement and sleep), and the sand is everything else (checking email, returning a call, dealing with nonurgent things). Don't get stuck in the sand. Here's an exercise to help you do that:

Plan to set aside thirty minutes every Sunday night for your weekly check-in and ask yourself this powerful question: "What goals do I need to accomplish in the next seven days for me to feel this week was a success?" List today's ten biggest marbles here and keep them at top of mind:

1. _____

2. _____

3. _____

4. _____

5. _____

6. _____

7. _____

8. _____

9. _____

10. _____

Now, think about what might make up some of your sand that could distract you from those important marbles. List your sand and think about how you can lessen that load:

_____

_____

_____

GET PLAYFUL

Although crossword puzzles are not as useful for preserving brain function as you might think (and you cannot expect any brain games to be the savior that many assume they are for your brain health), that doesn't mean there's no value at all in completing them and other word and numbers games like Wordle and Sudoku. Brain teasers in general can serve a function in stimulating your brain, improving working memory, and sharpening mental function. And they can be plain fun and stress reducing too. Brain games can be an escape pad from the rigors of everyday life. Seek out some puzzles this week and find ones that help you further get into a flow of sorts.

You can play video games too, but do so with other people and go 3D when you can. Games in 3D have actually been shown to help with planning and memory skills. And you don't have to seek out games designed for adults. Kids' video games can be just as engaging and challenging, especially complex ones that are fast-paced, action-packed, and get increasingly difficult as you play. So get your game on![17]

Another option is an online program from AARP, Staying Sharp, including a cognitive and lifestyle assessment, fun activities, interactive challenges, videos, and games. Visit aarp.org /brainhealth.

MUSIC

Music has always been a big part of my life. My parents, who were recent immigrants at the time, brought their love of Bollywood to the United States, and most of the music from those movies featured an accordion. For several years, I took accordion lessons. My parents thought it would be great if their son could one day play those same tunes, though most of what I learned were traditional German and Polish songs. Still, a love for music was born. In college, I sang in the glee club and now have playlists for just about every occasion.

Recently, I had a long conversation with Dr. Charles Limb, a friend and fellow neuroscientist, about music.[18] He has been studying the brains of jazz and improvisation artists, and his findings are remarkable. He found when musicians traded four bar blues, an improvisational method, the brain lit up as if in the middle of a very visual conversation. (When two musicians alternate short solos, this is called "trading fours.") Even more importantly, areas of the brain such as the dorsolateral prefrontal cortex became inhibited. This is a part of your brain that acts as a self-censor, and with less activity there, your brain relies more on its default network, which means your brain is freer to experiment, dream, and get into your zone or flow state (see Week 10). Charles told me that simply listening to that sort of music, with its improv riffs, can enhance your creativity. That is why my "thinking" music—music I like to hear when I'm concentrating—has a lot of jazz. Such a playlist is all instrumental and most songs tend to be around 120 beats per minute. Experiment with different types of jazz to find the one that resonates with you and your brain. Unless you're a musician, you probably won't start counting beats—let the beats speak to you and roll with whatever tunes seem to put you into a more relaxed, creative, and less inhibited state. Below are some accomplished artists to check out that you might find helpful in decompressing and getting into a more relaxed state; see which ones speak to you:

Louis Armstrong	Ella Fitzgerald
Chet Baker	Billie Holiday
Gary Burton	Diana Krall
Betty Carter	John LaPorta
John Coltrane	Pat Metheny
Harry Connick Jr.	Charles Mingus
Miles Davis	Thelonious Monk
Duke Ellington	Frank Sinatra
Bill Evans	Ben Webster

Don't think you have to play an instrument yourself or know how to read music to benefit. When I moderated the 2020 meeting of the Global Council on Brain Health, it had just released positive findings on the power of music on brain health.[19] And as Charles reminded me, music contributes to our well-being. It's a robust stimulus for the brain. Music is a universal language that conveys emotion. "It improves our empathy," Charles told me.

"It improves our ability to not feel alone and I think can help heal us in ways that a very fractured globe right now could really benefit from."

And don't underestimate the power of something as silly and fun as karaoke. My parents are big into karaoke. The word means "empty orchestra" in Japanese, but there's a release of endorphins and well-being neurotransmitters when you get up there and belt out a tune you know even though you can't sing like a pro. It's joyful and another opportunity to have a social experience. There's an upside to shutting off that self-conscious, self-monitoring part of your brain and allowing your walls to come down.

MUSIC FOR MY MIND

Create your own playlist here. Write down tunes you love to listen to when you're trying to focus on something important to complete a brain-demanding task. Aim for a good ten tunes:

_____

_____

_____

_____

_____

_____

_____

_____

_____

WEEK 6 NOTES

What I found helpful: _____

_____

What I found difficult: _____

_____

What I can improve upon: _____

_____

How I'm feeling in one to three words: _____

_____

Added Challenge: Ignore emails first thing in the morning (say, until 10:00 a.m.). Mornings are golden time. Use them to do your most creative work as opposed to procedural. As a super challenge: Take a break from social media this week. And to cap this week off, go back to page 120 where you wrote down ideas for de-stressing. Add to that list here:

_____

_____

_____

FIND YOUR FLOW

We've all experienced being "in the moment," "in the groove," or "on fire." *Flow* is the word used to describe this phenomenon, coined by the late social theorist Mihaly Csikszentmihalyi. It means you're in a mental state that has you totally immersed in an activity without distraction or any sense of agitation. You're deeply focused, enjoying a feeling of intense energy as you're absorbed in the activity. You're not necessarily stressed; rather, you can feel blissfully relaxed while at the same time being challenged or "under the gun." The concept of flow has been recognized across many fields, including occupational therapy, the arts, and the sports world. Mihaly may have given us the popular term in modern times, but the concept of flow has existed for thousands of years under other guises, notably in some Eastern religions.

What's the relationship between flow and brain health? You can't truly be in the flow without a clear sense of purpose. And we know that having purpose—leading a purpose-driven life—is essential to keeping the brain sharp. With purpose comes curiosity, exploration, discovery, new knowledge, unexpected but welcome challenges—all the things we know help boost the brain's networks and overall functionality.[20] Remember the study I pointed out in Part One: A sense of purpose has been shown to be associated with a 19 percent reduced rate of clinically significant cognitive impairment. It was no small study; it included 62,250 people across three continents with an average age of sixty. What was even more surprising was finding that the connection between brain health and purpose is even greater than other constructs like optimism and happiness. Your brain's physical health now and in the future rests more on your sense of meaning to life than your general outlook or feelings of contentment. The thinking is that when you live with purpose, you're more likely to engage in other protective behaviors such as maintaining a socially and physically active life. You're also more likely to pursue other brain-boosting activities like volunteering or practicing altruism. And let's be honest: Leading a purposeful life feels good. So get your groove on and see if you can find your flow this week.

Where to look? You might find it at work, or maybe not. Finding your flow doesn't have to be just about what you do for a living. You can achieve it in various ways through different experiences be they for professional or purely personal reasons. Think about the last time you were in the groove. How can you tell? Here are five hints:

- When you lost track of time.

- When you didn't have to think too hard to make progress in an endeavor.

- When you weren't interrupted by extraneous thoughts.

- When a task at hand seemed effortless.

- When you felt fully present in the moment.

So, what were you doing? How long has it been since that time? Who were you with? What describes the environment you were in?

I encourage you to write down those experiences here. They may inspire you to find new roads to flow this week.

_____

_____

_____

_____

_____

_____

_____

_____

_____

_____

_____

_____

FIND YOUR IKIGAI

Ikigai (ee-key-guy) is a word heard a lot in Japan, especially in Okinawa, where certain populations have incredibly low rates of dementia. Roughly translated, it means your reason for being. Ikigai is an ancient Japanese philosophy that has been a staple of Japanese culture. Some people believe it's largely the reason for their high levels of reported happiness and longevity. I think of it as the thing that makes me want to jump out of bed in the morning . . . and keeps me going all day. We would all do well to define our ikigai, because it is a daily reminder of our purpose here on earth. It's often used to help people define what they should be doing in their life by highlighting what they love, what they're good at, what they can get paid for, and what the world needs. But it also can be used more generally to solve lots of life's equations. Below is a popular visual image reflecting what ikigai entails:

Use the blank template below and write in words that reflect your ikigai.

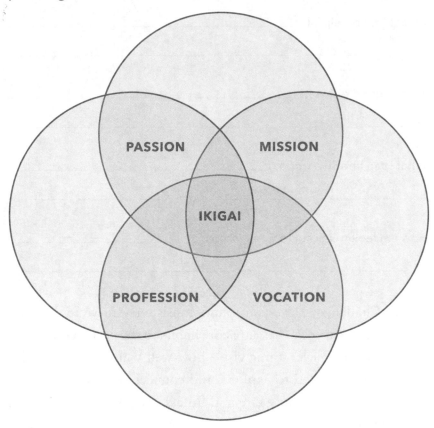

He who has a Why to live for can bear almost any How.

—Friedrich Nietzsche

WEEK 7 NOTES

What I found helpful: _____

_____

What I found difficult: _____

_____

What I can improve upon: _____

_____

How I'm feeling in one to three words: _____

_____

Added Challenge: Have you found consistency in your diet and exercise regimen yet? These are core habits to the entire enterprise, as they play into everything else—how well you sleep, cope with stress, feel motivated to explore, and connect with other people. Check in with your daily fare and fitness patterns and make sure you're living up to the promises you've made to yourself.

DO SOMETHING THAT SCARES YOU (EVERY DAY)

As you might have already guessed, this is my favorite dictum: "Do something that scares you (every day)." A version of this quote is often attributed to Eleanor Roosevelt, who was not referring to skydiving or watching a slasher movie. This adage is not meant to encourage excessive risks, but rather serve as a reminder to get out of your comfort zone and do things that make you a bit uncomfortable and push your limits. We are really good at doing the comfortable, easy, familiar, and predictable things; and there is something to be said for continuously practicing those habits (nearly half of our actions are habitual). But just as we delightfully surprise our bodies with new movements and routines, we should do the same for our brains. Science shows why doing something that (safely) scares you helps your brain, as it taps different areas of the neural network and can even promote the release of feel-good hormones.

I know I debunked the old myth that we only use 10 percent of our brains, but what is closer to the truth is that most of us probably employ only 10 percent of our brains 90 percent of the time! Think of it like this. We use our brains the way we probably lived our Covid lives—mostly at home with a few trips to the grocery store, school, and pharmacy. Our brains can stay on autopilot most of the time and avoid new or challenging things unless we push ourselves. If you start to focus on new activities outside your typical patterns, and embrace challenges that you know will be good for you, you have an opportunity to use different parts of your brain and maybe grow new brain cells in the process. A recent study from Oxford and Cambridge reveals that forced experimentation confers benefits, yet we all have a natural reluctance to experiment.[21] That's a shame when you think about it, because in many cases the risk of trying something new is relatively small, while the rewards can be enormous.

And get this: MIT's Dr. Earl K. Miller, a professor and researcher of neuroscience who studies how we carry out goal-directed behavior using complex mental processes and cognitive abilities, teaches that when you start doing the things you're afraid of or that make you nervous, your fear fades away.[22] Ask anyone near death what they regret the most and they will tell you that it wasn't what they did—it's what they didn't do! So, come on and take a chance. Sometimes the best moments in life come from doing the things that scare us the most. Even if you stumble or epically fail at first, it can be the initial step to success.

Every day this week, I want you to do something out of your usual norm or comfort zone, assuming it's safe and does not dampen or diminish your quality of life. Below are a few ideas, along with space for you to document your "scary" moments on pages 145–146:

❏ Talk to a stranger.

❏ Avoid all social media.

❏ Write a letter to your younger self.

❏ Write a letter to your older self.

❏ Cook a new food or cuisine.

❏ Call an estranged friend.

- ❑ Take a different route to work.
- ❑ Volunteer your time at a local soup kitchen or charity.
- ❑ Decline an invitation or request that will sap your energy.
- ❑ Sign up for an improv class.
- ❑ Go to a museum.
- ❑ Start a book club.
- ❑ Shop in a new market or retail store.
- ❑ Get a dog.
- ❑ Sit by a lakeside or oceanside beach for an hour reading a book.
- ❑ Get a massage.
- ❑ Plant a garden.
- ❑ Write the first page of your memoir.
- ❑ Plan a vacation to an exotic location.
- ❑ Seek a new job.
- ❑ Hire an intern to mentor.
- ❑ Forgive someone who wronged you.
- ❑ End a bad relationship.
- ❑ Renovate a room.
- ❑ Take a staycation for a night in a nice hotel nearby.
- ❑ De-clutter a closet or garage.
- ❑ Let yourself daydream.
- ❑ Try a coloring book for adults.
- ❑ Go sailing or fishing or try some other water sport.
- ❑ Explore a new town or area within driving distance from home.
- ❑ Change your signature.
- ❑ If you smoke, start a smoking cessation program.
- ❑ Move to a new city (at least think about it).

THE POWER OF FORGIVENESS

If you can't think of anything profound, I'll give you one that I listed above: Forgive someone who wronged you. Forgiveness has been shown to be a powerful promoter of mental and physical health that can reduce anxiety, depression, and major psychiatric disorders.[23] More upsides include reduced substance abuse, higher self-esteem, and greater life satisfaction—all good things for a happy brain. According to a survey by the nonprofit Fetzer Institute, fully 62 percent of American adults say they want more forgiveness from others in their personal lives (and this number increased to 83 percent in their communities, 90 percent in America, and 90 percent in the world).[24] There's nothing healthful about holding grudges, suppressing anger, and dwelling on negative thoughts and emotions. Granted, forgiving people can be hard. But hard things matter. Learn to let go. See if you can find someone to forgive and make that transaction happen this week. And try to practice small acts of forgiveness just by letting go of other people's transgressions that irk you and probably raise your blood pressure. For example, when someone is rude to you, or cuts you off in traffic, forgive them on the spot silently in your head and move on. After all, sometimes we take things too personally and overreact to our detriment. Free yourself of these unnecessary reactions.

Day 1 Scary moment: _____

Day 2 Scary moment: _____

Day 3 Scary moment: _____

Day 4 Scary moment: _____

Day 5 Scary moment: _____

Day 6 Scary moment: _____

Day 7 Scary moment: _____

One more idea to consider along these "scary" lines: One day every week I will get ready in the morning—shower, shave, brush my teeth, get dressed (including a tie)—with my eyes closed. I know that sounds crazy, but you should try it! It forces you to not only use all your other senses but also create strong visualizations in your brain built off the memory of where your clothes are located and recall the motor movements of getting dressed.

WEEK 8 NOTES

What I found helpful: _____

_____

What I found difficult: _____

_____

What I can improve upon: _____

_____

How I'm feeling in one to three words: _____

_____

Added Challenge: Take one of your scary moments and write about it here:

_____

_____

_____

_____

_____

_____

_____

How did it make you feel? What were the circumstances? What did you learn and how did it surprise you? How did it motivate you to think of other ways you can create more "scary moments"?

_____

_____

_____

_____

TAKE NOTE, TROUBLESHOOT, AND EDIT

What's working for you on this program so far? What's not? Below you'll get a chance to record some of your favorite tools you've enjoyed so far, as well as consider what weak spots remain in fully respecting the 6 pillars. But first, it's important to acknowledge that we all go through phases in life that bring different challenges. With each passing year and decade comes transitions punctuated by events like the birth of children, the death of loved ones, shifts in relationships, changes in our finances, retirement, accidents, illness, perhaps the loss of some independence such as the ability to drive. People who can adapt to life-changing circumstances and experiences are more likely to maintain their mental well-being. Never-ending sadness or stress is not a normal response to these transitions and raises the risk for cognitive impairment. It's important that you do what you can to keep track of your mental well-being and continuously strengthen your resilience. Use the prompts on these pages to take note of your feelings and see if you can tweak certain things in your life and habits to address problems.

My top three stressors are: _____
_____ .

I worry the most about (what keeps me up at night): _____
_____ .

One thing I can do this week to ease my anxiety is to: _____
_____ .

My life would be more fulfilling and joyful if: _____
_____ .

One thing I want to check off my bucket list soon: _____
_____ .

In Week 6, I spoke on the need to be more like a surgeon with your day by focusing on one task at a time. A part of that important lesson is to learn how to say "No" more often and not give in to the pressure to be and do everything. It's not good for the brain. As a colleague reminded me, "No" can be a complete sentence. The challenge, though, is to say "No" *without apologizing* and *without giving a reason.* You are not obligated to always justify why you are saying "No" to something. Don't worry: You can still be kind when you say it. Here are some ideas. Circle the ones you can memorize for the next time you need the line.

- No, that won't work for me.
- I'm not in a position to commit to that right now.
- Thanks for the invitation but I have other plans.
- Thanks for thinking of me but I must decline.

- Perhaps some other time but for now the answer is no.

- I appreciate the offer but unfortunately I'm not available.

  And if you need to simply press pause, say something like:

- Let me get back to you about that.

- Give me time to think about it and I'll circle back later.

- Oh, that sounds lovely but something I should consider at a later time, thanks.

Saying "No" does more than help free yourself up to do the things you want to do. It helps build confidence, ease stress, lower anxiety, and give your brain more room to grow and be creative. It de-clutters your psyche and establishes the kinds of boundaries you need to take care of *you*.

Speaking of care, I want you to go back now and see if there are areas in your life that are working well for you and those that continue to sabotage your mission to optimize your brain across all 6 pillars.

Nutrition

Favorite staples: _____

Weak spots: _____

Movement (Not Just "Exercise")

Favorite workouts: _____

Weak spots: _____

Downtime (in Waking Hours)

Favorite relaxation practices: _____

Weak spots: _____

Restorative Sleep

Favorite bedtime ritual: _____

Weak spots: _____

Discovery

Favorite new thing to do: _____

Weak spots: _____

Connection

Favorite people to hang out with: _____

Weak spots: _____

SYNCHING A CIRCADIAN RHYTHM

If you're not feeling like your body is loving you back despite all your efforts, it may be that your circadian rhythm is off balance. Dr. Satchin Panda is a respected researcher and scientist at the Salk Institute for Biological Studies who knows a thing or two about honoring the body's physiological clock. He's a staunch advocate for syncing our habits with our unique circadian rhythm. Every one of us has a circadian rhythm that includes our sleep-wake cycle, the rise and fall of hormones, and the fluctuations of body temperature that all correlate with the solar day. Your body's cells can tell time, so to speak, and your cells' "timetables" are present in every cell of every organ, including your brain. And this special body clock is controlled by an area in the brain's hypothalamus called the suprachiasmatic nucleus—it's your clockmaster.

Your circadian rhythm repeats roughly every twenty-four hours, but if it is not synchronized properly with the solar day, you won't feel 100 percent (ahem: It's the main cause of jet lag). What's more, you will increase your risk for many diseases from metabolic ones to heart disease, dementia, and cancer. Although your rhythm revolves mainly around your sleep habits, your other habits like what and when you eat and when you move can also have an impact. A healthy rhythm directs normal hormonal and enzymatic secretion patterns, from those associated with hunger cues and digesting food to those that relate to stress, cellular recovery, and even brain chemicals.

All the strategies in this workbook are designed to help you reset and recalibrate a broken rhythm, but if you're not feeling the love by this week, you may want to take more aggressive action and use an app that can help you further track your sleep. Many apps are available today to help you tailor your habits to your health and fine-tune everything so your rhythm is in prime shape for your body's peak performance. Experiment with a few of them.

Although we all share definite patterns—our greatest cardiovascular efficiency and muscle strength, for instance, peaks in late afternoon—note that everyone's rhythm will be slightly different and will respond differently to your daily habits. For some people, rigorous exercise late in the day will hinder a good night's sleep, but for other people a late-day sweat session can be sleep-enhancing. Get to know your personal circadian code and leverage the "power of when" to do the things you need to do. This will help you optimize your entire biology from the brain to blood sugar control to maintaining balance on your feet. Timing is everything! Respect your clock.

A human body can think thoughts, play a piano, kill germs, remove toxins, make a baby all at once. Once it's doing that, your biological rhythms are actually mirroring the symphony of the universe because you have circadian rhythms, seasonal rhythms, tidal rhythms [that] mirror everything that is happening in the whole universe.

—Theoretical physicist Michio Kaku

KEEP YOUR NUMBERS IN CHECK

As described in Part One, preventing and even slowing the progression of a neurodegenerative ailment will be increasingly reliant on precision medicine that can attune therapies to your unique physiology. There will come a day, for instance, when you can track biomarkers for neurodegeneration in your blood and use digital therapeutics to follow your risk for problems over time using software on your smartphone. Until we have that kind of technology available, it's important to stay on top of important "vital signs" of overall health, many of which play into risk for brain dysfunction and disease. To this end, I ask:

Are you up-to-date on your blood work, cancer screenings, and general checkups with your doctor? If not, schedule an appointment and make your health a priority this week. If you have any concerns about your cognitive abilities, bring them up with your doctor. Data from the U.S. Centers for Disease Control and Prevention suggests that nearly 13 percent of Americans reported experiencing worsening confusion or memory loss after age sixty, but most—fully 81 percent—had not consulted with a health care provider about their cognitive issues. Below is a list of a few metrics you'll want to keep abreast of and address any signs of abnormality:

- Blood pressure

- Fasting cholesterol and inflammation markers (e.g., C-reactive protein)

- Fasting blood sugar and diabetes screening (e.g., A1C)

And don't forget to keep up with immunizations, eye health, skin health, and dental health (see Added Challenge).

Be sure to keep your hearing in check too. According to the 2020 *Lancet* commission report on dementia prevention, intervention, and care that I mentioned earlier, hearing loss is now listed as one of the top risk factors for dementia. Research from Johns Hopkins finds that mild hearing loss doubles dementia risk, moderate loss triples risk, and people with a severe hearing impairment are five times more likely to develop dementia.[25] The reasons for the connection are multidimensional; hearing loss accelerates atrophy of the brain and contributes to social isolation, which then plays into a faster rate of cognitive decline. Nearly 27 million Americans over the age of fifty have hearing loss, but only one in seven uses a hearing aid. If you think your hearing has diminished, it's worth making an appointment with an audiologist for a hearing check. The good news is there are practical solutions to consider, from inconspicuous hearing aids (many of which are now available over the counter at lower costs) to cochlear implants that will rescue your hearing and save your brain. Don't delay.

LISTEN TO YOUR BODY

Your body is different every single day. No matter how fit and healthy you are, there will be times when you feel off. Even your body's overall status and functionality changes on an hourly basis. The profile of your microbiome will be different in the afternoon depending on what you ate in the morning. Sometimes I can't run the last mile or swim another lap in my workout routine. Other times, when I feel great, I can easily go an extra mile or lap without any problem. Don't beat yourself up on the days you need to dial it back. Listen to your body; it will tell you what it needs.

WEEK 9 NOTES

What I found helpful: _____

_____

What I found difficult: _____

_____

What I can improve upon: _____

_____

How I'm feeling in one to three words: _____

_____

Added Challenge: Floss twice daily this week if you don't already maintain a daily practice. Dental health is a lot more related to brain health than you can imagine. When I spoke with internationally renowned psychiatrist and aging expert Dr. Gary Small, founding former director of the UCLA Longevity Clinic and now Chair of Psychiatry at Hackensack University Medical Center in New Jersey, he stressed the importance of clearing out that debris between teeth. Flossing and brushing your teeth twice daily removes food residue and bacteria buildup that can ultimately lead to gum disease and increase risk of stroke. The connection to the brain? Gum disease entails inflammation. Periodontitis is an infection of the gums, the soft tissue at the base of the teeth, and the supporting bone. As the natural barrier between the tooth and gum erodes, bacteria from the infection have an entry into the bloodstream. Those bacteria can increase plaque buildup in the arteries, perhaps leading to clots. Hence, flossing is a good-for-brain habit.

A SPECIAL NOTE FOR
LONG COVID PATIENTS

I didn't address Covid-19 in *Keep Sharp* because the pandemic began after the book went to press. But we all know that the infection has caused millions of people who have survived it to suffer both short- and long-term consequences, many of which scientists are still trying to understand. Persistent symptoms, including brain fogginess, are not unique to Covid. They have been documented in the medical literature going back to 1889 related to the flu. And today, people who've been infected with other germs, such as those that cause Lyme disease or mononucleosis, can also experience persistent effects that involve many systems in the body, including the immune and nervous systems. And such effects can come to define a person's life.

Long-haul recovery programs are appearing throughout the country and at places like Mount Sinai Hospital in New York where a post-Covid clinic has been established. When Diana Berrent launched Survivor Corps in spring 2020 to help mobilize and collect data and research tools for patients and doctors alike, she didn't expect the following to grow so fast. But it's a testament to the problem and the ever-expanding need for answers and treatments. Berrent was among the first people to contract Covid in New York back in March 2020. She went on to have long-haul symptoms for months after testing negative for the virus, with those symptoms ranging from headaches and stomach issues to glaucoma, increasing her risk for blindness. Her preteen son also contracted the virus and still had symptoms nine months later.

Many people who develop long Covid didn't have a particularly severe experience with the virus when they were initially infected, and most survivors do not fit the stereotypical profile of people we'd expect to have a bad outcome with Covid. They are young. They are fit. They are high school sports stars, adults in their prime with no previous health problems or preexisting conditions, professional athletes, special operations military personnel, and doctors themselves. They cannot make sense of their body's roller-coaster reaction to Covid. Although women seem to be more at risk for long-haul Covid, we cannot dismiss the outliers to that pattern who are part of this conversation and whose experience will add to our knowledge and library of Covid medicine.

My advice to anyone suffering from long Covid is to find one of these post-Covid clinics near you that bring together specialists across the board—pulmonary, cardiology, and neurology. Make it a "family affair" in medicine and at home. This takes a multidisciplinary group approach to cover the panoply of syndromes. Survivor Corps (SurvivorCorps.com) is a great gateway for resources even if you don't live near New York. The site is easy to navigate and features live webinars, an events calendar, and a library of useful information. It is worth noting that many long-haulers have found relief through vaccination, which is great news and another reason to get vaccinated and stay on top of booster shots in the future. If you're a Covid survivor who still suffers, make this your week to address this unique challenge and become part of the solution by connecting with medical and scientific research efforts. Your brain—and whole body—will thank you.

GET REAL AND
HAVE A PLAN

By this point in your journey, you've begun to put the 6 pillars into practice through a combination of strategies. This week may seem like a slight detour but I hope you continue to execute those newly minted habits as you face this week's major task: putting your affairs in order. No one can promise anyone a lifetime of perfect brain health, so it helps to be as prepared as possible for the what-ifs. Each one of us at some point will know someone who is living with a form of dementia, be it a family member, friend, or oneself. The diagnosis will likely be the most devastating that person has ever received. As we are painfully aware of, there are no guaranteed cures for dementia and it's not easily treatable. The diagnosis can take a crushing toll on a family, with deep emotional, financial, and physical costs for the patient and caregivers. But a diagnosis needn't be a dead end. Many people can find renewed purpose and a zest for life after a diagnosis even when the future can feel like the great unknown that involves a lot of uncertainty. The key to dealing with those unknowns and uncertainties, however, is to plan well in advance and be as prepared as possible while you still have your faculties.

I know, it's not the conversations we like to have—the ones about grim diagnoses and death. But they are necessary if we want to be prepared for unfortunate events that can—and will—

happen. Do you have a will? A trust? A sense of how you'd like to be cared for should you receive a life-threatening diagnosis? Who will be in charge of your health and well-being? What will happen to you should you become sick or disabled?

If you haven't gotten around to it yet, you're not alone: The majority of Americans don't have a legal estate plan that includes clear directions under difficult circumstances and end-of-life decisions. But the need is there, especially when it comes to someone with brain decline. The 6 pillars you've begun to follow through a variety of strategies contribute to your "brain trust," but you also need to think about legal trusts of sorts to protect your family. This is true regardless of any potential brain ailment in the future but becomes essential when and if any diagnosis comes in.

There are numerous casualties when it comes to neurodegenerative diseases. Not only does the individual patient suffer; so does everyone else around him or her—from family members and friends to additional caregivers. It's emotionally and physically draining in addition to the cost in time and money. The stress that illness places on a family can be so burdensome that caregivers become "invisible second patients," with an increased risk for decline, depression, and brain disease. Caregivers of spouses with dementia are up to six times more likely to develop dementia than people in the general population.[26] And chronic inflammation that accompanies the anxiety and strain of caregiving further puts one at risk for every degenerative disease we know of today, from heart disease to cancer.

Clearly, the whole point of this workbook is to avoid such a fate, and neurodegenerative disease is not always inevitable. But we also must be realistic about the possibility of a diagnosis in our families and prepare for a worst-case scenario long in advance. If you take care of your will and trust—putting your affairs in order now—you can minimize fears, allay worries and future anxieties, and ultimately help yourself focus on the steps necessary to manage your own brain health.

Anyone with a brain needs to be thinking
about the possibility of Alzheimer's disease.

—Maria Shriver

This week is about taking inventory of your family's legal documents—wills, medical directives, and trusts at a minimum, but you may also want to explore other documents too such as life insurance and long-term-care policies. Talk to your family members and involve them in the process. These can be tough and awkward conversations but they will leave you and your loved ones feeling empowered and connected. For starters, if none of these important documents are in place, a family or estate attorney can help draft and execute them, which include things like durable power of attorney (designating who can make financial and other decisions when you are no longer able) and durable power of attorney for health care (designating who can make health care decisions when you are no longer able). These documents tend to be long and detailed because they specify some of the most practical but difficult decisions such as care facilities, types of treatment, end-of-life-care decisions (e.g., do you want feeding tubes?), and DNR (do not resuscitate) orders. Without instructions in place, expensive medical interventions are often routinely performed even if they are futile in extending life. To clarify, most standard wills and trusts detail how you'd like your assets distributed after your death. Medical or advance directives or *living* wills describe how end-of-life medical decisions are made according to your wishes.

CHECKLIST OF IMPORTANT DOCUMENTS TO HAVE:

❑ A living will or medical directive

❑ A durable power of attorney for health care (naming the person you want to make medical decisions for you)

❑ A durable power of attorney (naming the person you want to make your legal and financial decisions)

❑ A standard will

❑ A trust

Note: A living trust pools your assets into one entity, the trust, so your family can avoid the long and often costly probate process the courts use to distribute your assets after your death. Living trusts and wills are usually drafted together as a package.

You'll also want to organize assets, debts, insurance policies, and existing benefits like Medicare, retirement, and Social Security. The Financial and Legal Document Worksheet on the Alzheimer's Association's website can help you in your inventory, as well as resources provided by the National Institutes of Health's Advanced Care Planning website (see below). Two books you'll also find helpful: *Checklist for My Family: A Guide to My History, Financial Plans, and Final Wishes* (from AARP and the American Bar Association); and *The Other Talk: A Guide to Talking with Your Adult Children about the Rest of Your Life* (from AARP and McGraw Hill).

If this part of the planning feels overwhelming and uncomfortable or you're dealing with a complicated family estate, it helps to bring in a licensed and certified financial or legal advisor to be your guide. Be sure to choose this person carefully—preferably someone who has helped many families with eldercare and long-term-care planning.

I can't emphasize this enough: Don't wait for a diagnosis to make plans for the future. Start today. You are never too young or too old to get your affairs in order. Build your support network, ask for and accept help, and continually plan for the future, adjusting plans as needed, while accepting uncertainty.

STEPS FOR GETTING YOUR AFFAIRS IN ORDER

The following checklist is adapted from resources provided by the National Institute on Aging. I recommend you go there for useful tools and information you can download and print (see Added Challenge below for link). The site also clarifies a lot of confusing advice and offers plenty of answers to frequently asked questions.

- Store your important papers and copies of legal documents in one place. You can set up a file, put everything in a desk or dresser drawer, or list the information and location of papers in a notebook. If your papers are in a bank safe deposit box, keep copies in a file at home. Store digital files if you can or take pictures of key pages you can keep on a computer. Check every year to see if there's anything new to add or if you want to make any changes. Circumstances and family dynamics shift through the years and you'll want to keep things updated.

- Tell a trusted family member or friend where you put all your important papers. You don't need to tell this friend or family member about your personal affairs, but someone should know where you keep your papers in case of an emergency. If you don't have a relative or friend you trust, ask a lawyer to help. If you're the chief financial planner and bill payer in your household, you'll want someone you can trust to know where and how bills are paid in case you suddenly become incapacitated or otherwise unable to do your job.

- Discuss your end-of-life preferences with your family members and your doctor. He or she can explain what health decisions you may have to make in the future and what treatment options are available. Talking with your doctor can help ensure your wishes are honored. Discussing advance care planning decisions with your doctor is free through Medicare during your annual wellness visit. Private health insurance may also cover these discussions.

- Give permission in advance for your doctor or lawyer to talk with your caregiver. There may be questions about your care, a bill, or a health insurance claim. Without your consent, your caregiver may not be able to get necessary information. You can approve them as a representative to Medicare, credit card companies, your bank, and your doctor. You may need to sign and submit a form.

WEEK 10 NOTES

What I found helpful: _____

_____

What I found difficult: _____

_____

What I can improve upon: _____

_____

How I'm feeling in one to three words: _____

_____

Added Challenge: Go to the National Institutes of Health's Advanced Care Planning website (https://www.nia.nih.gov/health/getting-your-affairs-order#steps) and check out its resources, which include comprehensive lists of important papers, personal records, and legal documents you'll want to organize. The site also includes a list of additional resources you can trust, such as links and phone numbers to organizations that can help you complete this process. Do not be intimidated by this endeavor. It can be daunting, but it's empowering.

SELF-REFLECT

Practice makes progress, and we are all works in progress. But with each day come more potential and renewed promises for a better tomorrow. This week, use the following prompts to think about habits you'd like to keep or amend in pursuit of optimal brain function. Answers to some of these questions may overlap, and that's fine. Think deeply about your responses, and don't be alarmed if some of them surprise you. Take a few prompts a day at a time this week. If words don't seem to reflect your thinking, try pictures, images, photographs, or whatever helps you document the best answers to these crucial questions.

Although these questions may not seem to tie directly into brain health, they are part of a much bigger picture that encompasses your mental well-being. Some of your responses may inform new habits to practice that will help keep you sharp. Pay attention to your answers and see if they tell you further things you could be doing in the name of brain health. This exercise is a personal self-assessment of sorts that can provide clues to tailor this program to your own private self.

My favorite experiences and memories in life so far:

_____

_____

Things I'd like to forget:

_____

_____

Things I grieve:

_____

_____

What I value the most:

_____

_____

What I'd like to accomplish in the future:

_____

_____

Times I've overcome adversity:

_____

_____

All-time favorite songs:

_____

_____

Favorite recipes or meals:

_____

_____

What I love about my life:

_____

_____

What I'd like to change about my life:

_____

_____

Places I'd like to travel to and see:

_____

_____

New hobbies I'd like to try:

_____

_____

How I would define a beautiful life:

_____

_____

Where or how I see myself in one year:

_____

_____

Where or how I see myself in five years:

_____

_____

Where or how I see myself in ten years:

_____

_____

Ways I can make more time for myself:

_____

_____

*When one door closes another door opens; but we so often
look so long and so regretfully upon the closed door,
that we do not see the ones which open for us.*

—Alexander Graham Bell

As you go through this exercise, be particularly mindful of your inner dialogue. Are you sounding positive and upbeat about your wishes and desires? Or are you beating yourself up with pessimism and self-doubt? Do you find yourself looking in the rearview mirror with regret more than ahead with hope? The people I meet who keep sharp brains their entire lives are the individuals who see the glass as half-full despite challenges, setbacks, and disappointments. They look forward to the future with resolve, and don't spend too long reflecting on past mistakes and failures. They work on their happiness and take full ownership of their lives. What does taking ownership of your life—and your brain—mean to you? Write that down on the following page or draw a picture:

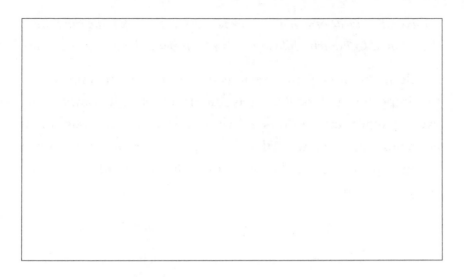

A positive attitude will go a long way to protect your brain. A good quotation has a way of consolidating your thoughts around a singular message and communicating that to other people. Below are three simple mantras of my own that I keep at the forefront of my brain, along with a gallery of affirmations you might want to consider for yourself:

"Do fewer things better"

This came from one of my first bosses in the media. He was referring to a tendency that many people have to try and include every aspect of a story in a television piece, which inadvertently overwhelms the viewer. He urged me to keep in mind that most people will probably grasp only a few concepts in a short piece of a few minutes. He taught me the importance of explaining those concepts well instead of trying to cram in every last fact. This quote is something I think about in other parts of my life as well. Sure, we would love to do it all, but sometimes there is tremendous joy in being able to do fewer things in a more thorough, complete, and, yes, better way.

"I would've written you a shorter letter, but I didn't have the time."
(attributed to French philosopher and mathematician Blaise Pascal)

Along the lines of the previous quote, this one reminds me of two important points. Brevity is important when it comes to delivering important messages. And crafting a concise message often takes more time and work than writing a longer one. It forces you to think, prioritize, and be judicious with your language, making every word count.

"Do something that scares you (every day)"

By now, you know this quote means so much to me. And I hope you enjoyed a lot of "scary" moments during Week 8. Have you kept up the habit and gotten out of your comfort zone at least once a day? Keep this mantra in your mind and think about ways you can live up to it. A little discomfort is part of learning new things and building cognitive reserve in the process.

Here are some fun affirmations to keep in mind:

I got this!

I am capable and worthy.

The world needs my gifts
and talents.

I am loved.

Things will work out.

I believe in myself.

I am resilient.

Anything is possible.

I am smart, kind, and joyful.

My life is beautiful.

Attitude is everything.

The best is yet to come.

My favorite personal mantras, affirmations, or quotes:

_____

_____

_____

_____

WEEK 11 NOTES

What I found helpful: _____

_____

What I found difficult: _____

_____

What I can improve upon: _____

_____

How I'm feeling in one to three words: _____

_____

Added Challenge: Choose a phrase or mantra that motivates you, sets your priorities, or lowers your stress. Frame a handwritten version of it to keep on your desk or someplace where you can see it throughout the day. Or just jot it down on a note and tape it up!

RINSE, RECYCLE, AND REPEAT

Can you believe it? You are in the final week. Time to take inventory of the changes you've made these past several weeks and ask yourself: What worked? What didn't work? Where can I improve? How can I take what I've just gone through to the next level?

Rinse away the habits you no longer want to keep, recycle the ones that will contribute to your brain's success, and repeat this program over and over again. Create nonnegotiables that you will commit to regularly, such as eating according to the S.H.A.R.P. plan, engaging in physical exercise every day, and being in bed at the same time every night.

Use this week to plan ahead. Your whole life is ahead of you. And you want that sharp brain to be with you as well. Remember to be flexible but consistent. When you momentarily stray from the program, don't be judgmental; simply get back on the path. Find goals that motivate you and write them down. It can be anything from teaching a skill you've developed in your life to planning an ecotour trip with your family. People who decide to focus on their health often do so for specific reasons, such as "I want to be more productive and have more energy," "I want to live longer without illness or disability," and "I don't want to die in the way my mother or father did." Always keep the big picture in mind.

This will help you not only maintain a healthy lifestyle but also get you back on track if you occasionally slip.

THE DECIDER RULE

When you find yourself at a crossroads when making decisions, especially big ones that might affect your future, try "The Decider Rule" to guide you. Here's what I mean by that: Imagine you're an old person sitting in your rocking chair. The majority of your life is behind you, and you've got a rich library of memories in your brain to recall and enjoy again. Those memories are like movie scenes you get to luxuriate in as you slowly reach the end of your life with grace and dignity. When trying to decide what to do or not do today, ask yourself: Is this a memory I will want to have when I'm old and basking in the glow of my history? That question is all you need to know whether to say No or Go.

MINI SELF-ASSESSMENT:

At this point, I encourage you to ask yourself the following questions:

- ❑ Am I following the S.H.A.R.P. nutritional protocol whenever possible?

- ❑ Am I getting at least thirty minutes of exercise or brisk movement at least five days a week and including strength or resistance training at least two days a week? Do my activities also work on flexibility, coordination, and balance?

- ❑ Am I managing stress better and feeling more resilient?

- ❑ Am I getting more restful sleep on a regular basis?

- ❑ Am I learning something new regularly that challenges my mind and demands developing different skills? Am I doing something every day that "scares" me?

- ❑ Am I connecting with friends and family members regularly while also expanding my fellowship universe?

If you cannot answer these questions in the affirmative, see if you can make changes to your lifestyle. What obstacles are blocking you? How can you overcome them? Write some down here with potential solutions:

_____

_____

_____

_____

_____

If you're still not getting results, it may be time to seek additional help. For example, if your sleep is still troubling you, ask your doctor about a sleep study and be sure medications you take are not interfering with your progress. If chronic stress is an issue or you think you might meet the definition of depression, seek a qualified psychiatrist or therapist.

Your environment is more important to how you build habits than anything else, including genes, so pay attention to it. When it comes to brain decline and disease, Alzheimer's included, we may never in our lifetime be able to rely on a miracle cure or preventive panacea through drugs to save us. However, what will save many of our brains from illness is a focus on prevention by taking what we can control within our environment to foster superior brain health. Take a look around you and where you spend the most time. Is it conducive to living a healthy life?

If you haven't tried to keep a gratitude journal yet or if you stopped writing down your grateful moments and accomplishments as you did during Week 6, return to that exercise. Each morning, spend five minutes making a list of at least five people or situations you are grateful for. If weather permits, do this outside in the fresh air and morning sunlight. If you repeat items on your previous list, that's okay. Think of things that happened the day before that can be added to the list. They can be as minor as being grateful that you felt pretty good and reached your goals for the day.

And as a final exercise, write a handwritten letter to a younger loved one in the family, describing something you've learned in your life that you can pass down as an important lesson. Draft your letter on the following page and create a final version on fancy paper to deliver.

A FINAL WORD OF
SHARP WISDOM

After the initial publication of *Keep Sharp*, I was struck by how many people truly enjoyed the work, especially those I didn't expect—individuals who, given their young age, I assumed didn't yet think about the future health of their brains. But change is afoot among younger generations who are indeed putting more effort into optimizing their lives and engaging in activities that will preserve their brain function. Sometimes it just takes an ill family member or personal brush with mortality to motivate someone to change. Much to my surprise, I also heard from esteemed mentors of mine who helped cultivate me as a doctor and neurosurgeon many decades ago, and who are now dealing with friends and family members in cognitive decline. It's deeply humbling to know I can reach such a wide spectrum of people and try to make a positive difference in their lives. May this mission of mine continue. I hope you join me in this mission by living up to your brain's fullest potential and enlisting others to follow your example.

A story I told in *Keep Sharp* is worth retelling here. When my father was just forty-seven years old, he developed crushing chest pain while out on a walk. I remember the panicked call I received from my mom, and the voice of the 911 operator I spoke to seconds later. A few hours later, he had an emergency four-vessel bypass operation on his heart. It was a frightening ordeal for our family, and we were worried he might not survive the operation. I was a young medical student at the time (not sleeping enough and probably relying too much on sugary snacks). As you can imagine, I was fairly convinced I had somehow failed him. After all, I should have seen the warning signs, counseled him on his health, and helped him avoid heart disease. Fortunately, he survived, and this event completely changed his life. He lost thirty pounds, paid close attention to the foods he was eating, and made regular movement a priority. His recovery made an impression on me, and I vowed to address things in my own life before they became mission critical. Now that I am past that age with my own children, I make it a priority to learn not just how to prevent disease but to continually assess myself to make sure I'm performing to the best of my ability.

My father worked for thirty-five years in the auto industry alongside my mom, who happened to be the first woman ever hired as an engineer by Ford Motor Company. No surprise: Everyone in my family loves car analogies. On the weekends during my childhood, we all tinkered with the family car. Our garage was filled with toolboxes and a running commentary about how the human body wasn't that much different from the Ford LTD we were rebuilding. Both had engines, pumps, and life-sustaining fuel. Upon recent reflection, I think those conversations contributed to my interest in the brain, because there was one area of the body that really couldn't be compared mechanically to a car. After all, there is no seat of consciousness in a car, no matter how plush the leather. Still, it is nearly impossible for me to look at the brain and not think about tuning up and maintenance. Is an oil change necessary? Is it getting the right fuel? Is it revving too high or being driven without a break for maintenance? Are there cracks in the windshield or the chassis, and do all the tires have enough air pressure? Can it heat and cool properly? Does the engine respond appropriately to a sudden demand for speed, and how quickly can it be brought to a halt? I think you can get my point.

Recently, I had a long conversation with my parents about cars and traffic. I told them about an interview I had done with Dr. Dwight Hennessy, who is a traffic psychologist, and Kayla Chavez, a long-haul truck driver who spends her days driving crazy distances across the country. It was a captivating segment for my podcast. First of all: Who knew there were people called traffic psychologists who take psychological principles and apply them to traffic situations? It fascinated me that few people—myself included—stop to think about how much the simple but complex act of driving a car affects us in life. Most people drive every day. It's how we move, meet other people, get to work and home, pick up items we need to survive, and so on. We bring certain attitudes, expectations, personalities, and perhaps frustrations to the task. For some, driving is the most stressful part of one's day and for others it's a peaceful time for self-reflection and relaxation. Driving has a physiological impact on us. Our heart rate, blood pressure, and respiration change. It can even shift our mood and cognition. For example, a driving experience that makes us agitated can also have the effect of making us less vigilant to things that are going on, more anxious and angry, and we may show up to our destination in a way that cripples our ability to work efficiently, collaborate with others, and generally take pleasure in the day.

Driving is one of the most dangerous actions we do. By the same token, it's among the most stimulating for our brain. There's so much we have to juggle and coordinate in our brains while on the road. So many split-second decisions to make, some of which are life-and-death. And yet we worry often about other things while driving! Kayla, the long-haul truck driver, told me she prefers to spend the first thirty minutes of her drive in silence. She doesn't put on any music or media and simply looks ahead and takes it all in—the natural beauty around her. I sensed she gains just as much pleasure from observing rich landscapes as she does passing billboards and barren land.

My whole point in bringing this up is to show how much driving parallels life itself and the pursuit of a sharp brain. Every one of us sits in the driver's seat. You can drive your car with whatever attitude and personality you want—patient and curious, or aggressive and angry. You can choose which road to take, how to respond to others, and how to spend the time as you go from point A to point B. You also get to choose which type of car to drive, how to care for it, and what driving style you'll force on it. I won't bore you with any more car analogies but I'll leave you with some final questions.

Where is your road taking you today? Are you caring for your body—the vehicle that's taking you? What do you want your brain's final destination to be? Are you willing to take the steps to have a safe trip and arrive in sharp condition? You can draw the map, create the roads, and settle into a method of driving to take you there. My hope is that you have fun. Enjoy the scenery. And may it be your own road less traveled that's more fulfilling than anything else in life.

ACKNOWLEDGMENTS

The scientists who wake up every morning with the belief that diseases are not preordained, that memory loss need not accompany aging, and that everyone can make their brains better inspired me to write this book. Over nearly two decades, I would speak to these scientists at the big brain meetings, in their laboratories, and in their homes. They would share their scientific findings but also let me in on the deeply personal reasons they had chosen to study the brain in the first place. They convinced me not only that we would one day make diseases like dementia a thing of the past, but that even a healthy brain could be improved and made more resilient. Thank you for your candor and your willingness to help take some of the most remarkable new knowledge about the brain and make it relevant for anyone, anywhere.

Priscilla Painton, executive editor is your title but it does not nearly begin to describe the role you played in the original Keep Sharp project, which then extended to this workbook thanks to your brilliant idea. From the beginning, your vision was clear and your collaboration far exceeded my expectations. Your remarks and notes were always spot-on, and always added great value. You have an ability to see around corners and anticipate the direction of a book. I have been fortunate to have such a dedicated and professional team helping me on this workbook, which was expertly led editorially by Hana Park and her team: Julia Prosser, Elizabeth

Herman, Yvette Grant, Jackie Seow, Marie Florio, Elizabeth Venere, Matthew Monahan, and Amanda Mulholland. Thanks to all of you.

Jonathan Karp, you are the definition of a gentleman and a scholar. I knew after the first meeting in your office, when we discussed everything from stem cells to Springsteen, that I was dealing with someone truly engaged with the world. Thanks for believing in me and the entire Keep Sharp project. Bob Barnett is a world-famous lawyer. He has represented presidents and the pope. Yet you would never know it. He is so incredibly humble and hardworking. One of the best days in my life was the day Bob Barnett agreed to help me with my career. His guidance has been remarkably prescient and insightful.

The collaboration I have had with my partner and friend, Kristin Loberg, has been truly special. We should all be lucky enough to have a real mind meld with someone like Kristin, who immediately understood what I was trying to convey and always helped me get there. She is the very best at what she does, and quite simply, this book would not have been possible without her.

REFERENCES

Below is a curated list of citations that accompany specific studies mentioned in the workbook. Remember too that *Keep Sharp* also includes notes. For general statements, I trust you can find a wellspring of sources and evidence yourself online with just a few taps of the keyboard, assuming you visit reputable sites that post fact-checked, credible information that's been vetted by experts. This is especially important when it comes to matters of health and medicine. Reputable medical journal search engines that do not require a subscription, many of which are listed in the notes, include: pubmed.gov (an online archive of medical journal articles maintained by the National Institutes of Health's National Library of Medicine); sciencedirect.com and its sibling SpringerLink; the Cochrane Library at cochranelibrary.com; and Google Scholar at scholar.google.com, which is a great secondary search engine to use after your initial search. The databases accessed by these search engines include Embase (owned by Elsevier), Medline, and MedlinePlus and cover millions of peer-reviewed studies from around the world. Studies often get published in advance online before formally being released in peer-reviewed journals. Lead authors are usually listed last.

INTRODUCTION

1 Nina E. Fultz et al., "Coupled Electrophysiological, Hemodynamic, and Cerebrospinal Fluid Oscillations in Human Sleep," *Science* 366, no. 6465 (November 2019): 628–31.

2 Elena P. Moreno-Jiménez et al., "Adult Hippocampal Neurogenesis Is Abundant in Neurologically Healthy Subjects and Drops Sharply in Patients with Alzheimer's Disease," *Nature Medicine* 25, no. 4 (April 2019): 554–60.

3 Shuntaro Izawa et al., "REM Sleep-Active MCH Neurons Are Involved in Forgetting Hippocampus-Dependent Memories," *Science* 365, no. 6459 (September 2019): 1308–13.

4 See: https://www.aarp.org/health/brain-health/global-council-on-brain-health/behavior-change/.

5 J. Graham Ruby et al., "Estimates of the Heritability of Human Longevity Are

REFERENCES

Substantially Inflated Due to Assortative Mating," *Genetics* 210, no. 3 (November 2018): 1109–24.

6 Céline Bellenguez et al., "New Insights into the Genetic Etiology of Alzheimer's Disease and Related Dementias," *Nature Genetics* 54, no. 4 (April 2022): 412–36.

7 Jianwei Zhu et al., "Physical and Mental Activity, Disease Susceptibility, and Risk of Dementia: A Prospective Cohort Study Based on UK Biobank," *Neurology* 10 (July 2022).

PART ONE

1 Sami El-Boustani et al., "Locally Coordinated Synaptic Plasticity of Visual Cortex Neurons in Vivo," *Science* 360, no. 6395 (June 2018): 1349–54.

2 See page 9 for discussion of cognitive plasticity. Global Council on Brain Health. "Engage Your Brain: GCBH Recommendations on Cognitively Stimulating Activities." Washington, DC: Global Council on Brain Health, July 2017. https://doi.org/10.26419/pia.00001.001.

3 Natalia Caporale and Yang Dan, "Spike Timing-Dependent Plasticity: A Hebbian Learning Rule," *Annual Review of Neuroscience* 31 (2008): 25–46.

4 Claudio Franceschi et al., "Inflammaging: A New Immune-Metabolic Viewpoint for Age-Related Diseases," *Nature Reviews Endocrinology* 14, no. 10 (October 2018): 576–90.

5 K. A. Walker, R. F. Gottesman, A. Wu, et al., "Systemic Inflammation During Midlife and Cognitive Change over 20 Years: The ARIC Study," *Neurology* 92, no. 11 (2019): e1256–e1267. Also see: R. F. Gottesman, A. L. Schneider, M. Albert, et al., "Midlife Hypertension and 20-Year Cognitive Change: The Atherosclerosis Risk in Communities Neurocognitive Study," *JAMA Neurology* 71, no. 10 (2014): 1218–27.

6 Gill Livingston et al., "Dementia Prevention, Intervention, and Care: 2020 Report of the Lancet Commission," *Lancet* 396, no. 10248 (August 2020): 413–46.

7 Joshua R. Ehrlich et al., "Addition of Vision Impairment to a Life-Course Model of Potentially Modifiable Dementia Risk Factors in the US," *JAMA Neurology* 79, no. 6 (June 2022): 623–26.

8 M. C. Morris, C. C. Tangney, Y. Wang, et al., "MIND Diet Associated with Reduced Incidence of Alzheimer's Disease," *Alzheimer's and Dementia* 11, no. 9 (2015): 1007–14.

9 Klodian Dhana et al., "MIND Diet, Common Brain Pathologies, and Cognition in Community-Dwelling Older Adults," *Journal of Alzheimer's Disease* 83, no. 2 (2021): 683–92.

10 See page 5 at https://www.aarp.org/content/dam/aarp/health/brain_health/2018/01/gcbh-recommendations-on-nourishing-your-brain-health.doi.10.26419%252Fpia.00019.001.pdf.

11 www.cdc.gov, "Get the Facts: Added Sugars," https://www.cdc.gov/nutrition/data-statistics/added-sugars.html.

12 Giuseppe Faraco et al., "Dietary Salt Promotes Cognitive Impairment through Tau Phosphorylation," *Nature* 574, no. 7780 (October 2019): 686–90.

13 Magdalena Miranda et al., "Brain-Derived Neurotrophic Factor: A Key Molecule for Memory in the Healthy and the Pathological Brain," *Frontiers in Cellular Neuroscience* 13 (August 2019): 363.

14 See JohnRatey.com.

15 Miranda et al., "Brain-Derived Neurotrophic Factor: A Key Molecule for Memory in the Healthy and the Pathological Brain."

16 Patricia C. García-Suárez et al., "Acute Systemic Response of BDNF, Lactate and Cortisol to Strenuous Exercise Modalities in Healthy Untrained Women," *Dose Response* 18, no. 4 (December 2020): 1559325820970818.

17 See: https://www.aarp.org/health/dementia/info-2022/exercise-slows-memory-loss.html. Also see: Daniel G. Blackmore et al., "An Exercise 'Sweet Spot' Reverses Cognitive Deficits of Aging by Growth-hormone-induced Neurogenesis," *iScience* 24, no. 11 (October 2021): 103275.

18 Anne-Julie Tessier et al., "Association of Low Muscle Mass with Cognitive Function During a 3-Year Follow-up Among Adults Aged 65 to 86 Years in the Canadian Longitudinal Study on Aging," *JAMA Network Open* 5, no. 7 (July 2022): e2219926.

19 Benjamin S. Olivari et al., "Population Measures of Subjective Cognitive Decline: A Means of Advancing Public Health Policy to Address Cognitive Health," *Alzheimer's & Dementia* (NY) 7, no. 1 (March 2021): e12142.

20 S. Beddhu, G. Wei, R. L. Marcus, et al., "Light-Intensity Physical Activities and Mortality in the United States General Population and CKD Subpopulation," *Clinical Journal of the American Society of Nephrology* 10, no. 7 (2015): 1145–53.

21 Global Council on Brain Health (2018). "Brain Health and Mental Well-Being: GCBH Recommendations on Feeling Good and Functioning Well." Available at www.GlobalCouncilOnBrainHealth.org. DOI: https://doi.org/10.26419/pia.00037.001.

22 For access to a library of resources and data about sleep, see the National Sleep Foundation's website: SleepFoundation.org. Also see: Global Council on Brain Health (2016). "The Brain-Sleep Connection: GCBH Recommendations on Sleep and Brain Health." Available at www.GlobalCouncilOnBrainHealth.org DOI: https://doi.org/10.26419/pia.00014.001.

23 S. M. Purcell, D. S. Manoach, C. Demanuele, et al., "Characterizing Sleep Spindles in 11,630 Individuals from the National Sleep Research Resource," *Nature Communications* 26, no. 8 (2017): 15930.

24 J. J. Iliff, M. Wang, Y. Liao, et al., "A Paravascular Pathway Facilitates CSF

REFERENCES

Flow Through the Brain Parenchyma and the Clearance of Interstitial Solutes, Including Amyloid β," *Science Translational Medicine* 4, no. 147 (2012): 147ra111.

25 Nina E. Fultz et al., "Coupled Electrophysiological, Hemodynamic, and Cerebrospinal Fluid Oscillations in Human Sleep," *Science* 366, no. 6465 (November 2019): 628–31.

26 Matthew Walker, *Why We Sleep: Unlocking the Power of Sleep and Dreams* (New York: Scribner, 2017).

27 C. Dufouil, E. Pereira, G. Chêne, et al., "Older Age at Retirement Is Associated with Decreased Risk of Dementia," *European Journal of Epidemiology* 29, no. 5 (2014): 353–61.

28 See: Global Council on Brain Health (2017). "Engage Your Brain: GCBH Recommendations on Cognitively Stimulating Activities." Available at: www.GlobalCouncilOnBrainHealth.org Engage Your Brain: GCBH Recommendations on Cognitively Stimulating Activities 2 DOI: https://doi.org/10.26419/pia.00001.001.

29 Georgia Bell et al., "Positive Psychological Constructs and Association with Reduced Risk of Mild Cognitive Impairment and Dementia in Older Adults: A Systematic Review and Meta-Analysis," *Ageing Research Reviews* 77 (May 2022): 101594.

30 See: Global Council on Brain Health (2017). "The Brain and Social Connectedness: GCBH Recommendations on Social Engagement and Brain Health." Available at www.GlobalCouncilOnBrainHealth.org.

31 "Loneliness and Social Isolation Linked to Serious Health Conditions," Public Health Media Library at www.cdc.gov. Also see: National Academies of Sciences, Engineering, and Medicine, *Social Isolation and Loneliness in Older Adults: Opportunities for the Health Care System.* Washington, DC: National Academies Press, 2020.

32 Julianne Holt-Lunstad et al., "Loneliness and Social Isolation as Risk Factors for Mortality: A Meta-analytic Review," *Perspectives on Psychological Science* 10, no. 2 (March 2015): 227–37.

33 https://www.adultdevelopmentstudy.org/.

PART TWO

1 H. J. Lee, H. I. Seo, H. Y. Cha, et al., "Diabetes and Alzheimer's Disease: Mechanisms and Nutritional Aspects," *Clinical Nutrition Research* 7, no. 4 (2018): 229–40. Also see: Fanfan Zheng, Li Yan, Zhenchun Yang, et al., "HbA1c, Diabetes and Cognitive Decline: The English Longitudinal Study of Ageing," *Diabetologia* 61, no. 4 (2018): 839–48; and N. Zhao, C. C. Liu, A. J. Van Ingelgom, and

Y. A. Martens, "Apolipoprotein E4 Impairs Neuronal Insulin Signaling by Trapping Insulin Receptor in the Endosomes," *Neuron* 96, no. 1 (2017): 115–29.e5.

2 Remi Daviet et al., "Associations Between Alcohol Consumption and Gray and White Matter Volumes in the UK Biobank," *Nature Communications* 13, no. 1 (March 2022): 1175.

3 Matthew C. L. Phillips, "Fasting as a Therapy in Neurological Disease," *Nutrients* 11, no. 10 (October 2019): 2501.

4 See: Global Council on Brain Health (2019). "The Real Deal on Brain Health Supplements: GCBH Recommendations on Vitamins, Minerals, and Other Dietary Supplements." Available at www.GlobalCouncilOnBrainHealth.org. DOI: https://doi.org/10.26419/pia.00094.001.

5 Line Jee Hartmann Rasmussen et al., "Association of Neurocognitive and Physical Function with Gait Speed in Midlife," *JAMA Network Open* 2, no. 10 (October 2019): e1913123.

6 Masahiro Okamoto et al., "High-intensity Intermittent Training Enhances Spatial Memory and Hippocampal Neurogenesis Associated with BDNF Signaling in Rats, *Cerebral Cortex* 31, no. 9 (July 2021): 4386–97; Cinthia Maria Saucedo Marquez et al., "High-intensity Interval Training Evokes Larger Serum BDNF Levels Compared with Intense Continuous Exercise," *Journal of Applied Physiology* 119, no. 12 (December 2015): 1363–73.

7 Peter Schnohr et al., "Various Leisure-Time Physical Activities Associated with Widely Divergent Life Expectancies: The Copenhagen City Heart Study," *Mayo Clinic Proceedings* 93, no. 12 (December 2018): 1775–85.

8 Ibid.

9 www.cdc.gov.

10 Min-Jing Yang et al., "Association of Nap Frequency with Hypertension or Ischemic Stroke Supported by Prospective Cohort Data and Mendelian Randomization in Predominantly Middle-Aged European Subjects," *Hypertension* 79, no. 9 (September 2022): 1962–70.

11 See: https://www.aarp.org/health/conditions-treatments/info-2020/computer-glasses-blue-light-protection.html?cmp=KNC-DSO-COR-Health-EyeStrain-Non Brand-Exact-28932-GOOG-HEALTH-ConditionsTreatments-ConditionsTreat ments-BlueLightGlasses-Exact-NonBrand&gclid=CjwK.

12 Peggy J. Liu et al., "The Surprise of Reaching Out: Appreciated More than We Think," *Journal of Personality and Social Psychology* (July 2022).

13 Ibid.

14 Gabrielle N. Pfund et al., "Being Social May Be Purposeful in Older Adulthood: A Measurement Burst Design," *American Journal of Geriatric Psychiatry* 30, no. 7 (July 2022): 777–86.

15 Kelsey D. Biddle et al., "Social Engagement and Amyloid-β-Related Cognitive

Decline in Cognitively Normal Older Adults," *American Journal of Geriatric Psychiatry* 27, no. 11 (November 2019): 1247–56. Also see: Matteo Piolatto et al., "The Effect of Social Relationships on Cognitive Decline in Older Adults: An Updated Systematic Review and Meta-Analysis of Longitudinal Cohort Studies," *BMC Public Health* 22, no. 1 (February 2022): 278.

16 Julianne Holt-Lunstad et al., "Loneliness and Social Isolation as Risk Factors for Mortality: A Meta-analytic Review," *Perspectives on Psychological Science* 10, no. 2 (March 2015): 227–37.

17 See: Global Council on Brain Health. "Engage Your Brain: GCBH Recommendations on Cognitively Stimulating Activities." Washington, DC: Global Council on Brain Health, July 2017. DOI: https://doi.org/10.26419/pia.00001.001.

18 See my podcast from June 7, 2022, "Sometimes It's Healthy to Break the Rules." Also see: Charles J. Limb and Allen R. Braun, "Neural Substrates of Spontaneous Musical Performance: An fMRI Study of Jazz Improvisation," *PLOS One* 3, no. 2 (February 2008): e1679.

19 See: "Music on Our Minds: The Rich Potential of Music to Promote Brain Health and Mental Well-Being." Available at www.GlobalCouncilOnBrainHealth.org. DOI: https://doi.org/10.26419/pia.00103.001.

20 Adam Kaplin and Laura Anzaldi, "New Movement in Neuroscience: A Purpose-Driven Life," *Cerebrum: The Dana Forum on Brain Science* (June 2015): 7.

21 Shaun Larcom, Ferdinand Rauch, and Tim Willems, "The Benefits of Forced Experimentation: Striking Evidence from the London Underground Network," *The Quarterly Journal of Economics* 132, no. 4 (November 2017): 2019–55.

22 Access Earl Miller's work and research papers at https://ekmillerlab.mit.edu/earl-miller/.

23 "Forgiveness: Your Health Depends on It," Johns Hopkins Medicine, https://www.hopkinsmedicine.org/health/wellness-and-prevention/forgiveness-your-health-depends-on-it.

24 https://fetzer.org/resources/resources-forgiveness.

25 "The Hidden Risks of Hearing Loss," Johns Hopkins Medicine, https://www.hopkinsmedicine.org/health/wellness-and-prevention/the-hidden-risks-of-hearing-loss#:~:text=In%20a%20study%20that%20tracked,more%20likely%20to%20develop%20dementia.

26 Maria C. Norton et al., "Increased Risk of Dementia When Spouse Has Dementia? The Cache County Study," *Journal of the American Geriatric Society* 58, no. 5 (2010): 895–900.

ABOUT THE AUTHOR

Sanjay Gupta fell in love with the brain as a young boy in middle school. He later went on to spend four years earning a medical degree and then seven years completing residency training so he could become a neurosurgeon—a practice he has been enjoying for the last twenty-some years. The brain is his first and truest love. Dr. Gupta is a multiple *New York Times* bestselling author and serves as the chief medical correspondent for CNN. Since 2001, Gupta has covered the biggest health headlines of our time—often telling the harrowing and touching stories of brave first responders, and reporting from the front lines of nearly every conflict, natural disaster, and disease outbreak anywhere in the world. He has hosted several long-form documentaries based on deep investigations, including his *Weed* series and *One Nation Under Stress* for HBO. For his work, he has achieved numerous Emmy and Peabody awards, as well as the DuPont award—the broadcast equivalent of the Pulitzer. Gupta is widely regarded as one of the most trusted reporters in the media. In addition to his accolades in journalism, Gupta is the recipient of several honorary degrees and has been recognized with many humanitarian awards for his care of people injured in wars and natural disasters. *Forbes* magazine named him one of the ten most influential celebrities.

In 2019, Gupta was elected to the National Academy of Medicine, one of the highest honors in the medical field. In 2022, he was inducted into the American Academy of Arts & Sciences. Gupta lives in Atlanta where he is also an associate professor of neurosurgery at Emory University Hospital and associate chief of neurosurgery at Grady Memorial Hospital. He serves as a diplomate of the American Board of Neurosurgery. Sanjay is married to Rebecca, who, after reading this, reminded him that she was in fact his truest love. He wisely conceded this point. They have three teenage daughters, who find it hilarious their father wrote a book about memory. As they put it, the Gupta Girls believe their father "literally can't remember anything."